Surfing Tommies

Alan M. Kent

Surfing Tommies

A Cornish Tragedy

Francis
Boutle
Publishers

First published by Francis Boutle Publishers
272 Alexandra Park Road
London N22 7BG
020 8889 7744
www.francisboutle.co.uk

ISBN 978 1 903427 48 4

Printed by Melita Press, Malta

BishBashBosh Productions

BISH BASH BOSH PRODUCTIONS

BishBashBosh Productions are a new production company from Cornwall dedicated to commissioning, developing and producing theatre, film and media – new work that offers a response to Cornish issues, trends and events. We find our inspiration in landscape, community, multi-culturalism, Celticity, and literature and theatre across frontiers. In this way we hope to develop a national theatre for Cornwall (Gwaryjy Kenedhlek rag Kernow).

Since 2007 we have produced critically-acclaimed productions in Cornwall, London and on tour, including *Oogly es Sin*, *The Tin Violin* and *A Mere Interlude*. We aim to develop new work through events, workshops, readings, research and literary programmes. Our remit is also within education, to work with students and teachers in and outside of Cornwall.

Surfing Tommies was awarded Development Funding from the Cultural Events Programme of the United Nations Educational, Scientific and Cultural Organization World Heritage Site of the Cornwall and West Devon Mining Landscape and is partly funded by Arts Council England.

For BishBashBosh Productions:

Patron	Benjamin Luxon
Artistic Directors	Dean Nolan and Alan M. Kent
Associate Artists	Victoria Guy, Trevor Cuthbertson, Molly Weaver, Mbuguah Goro, Joanne Clare, Ed Williams, Holly Kavanagh, Catherine Self, Benjamin Symes, Sally Crooks, Jamie Trotter, Victoria Guy, John Hoggarth and Ria Parry
Publisher	Francis Boutle Publishers

info@bishbashboshproductions.co.uk
www.bishbashboshproductions.co.uk
16 Hicks Close, Probus, Truro, Cornwall TR2 4NE

Iron Shoes

Iron Shoes is a production company formed by John Hoggarth and Ria Parry in 2009.

Iron Shoes is dedicated to making quality theatre that is engaging, honest and irresistible.

We are interested in telling stories that fire the imagination, stimulate the senses and inspire the soul.

Our first production *Crush* premiered at the Edinburgh Festival 2009, winning a Scotsman Fringe First Award. The production was also nominated for two Stage Awards and shortlisted for the Carol Tambor New York Award.

In 2010 *Crush* completed a national tour. We worked with Kids Taskforce to create *Watch Over Me Series 4*, a television education drama written by John Hoggarth, delivered to every secondary school in the country in partnership with the Home Office.

In March 2011 Iron Shoes produced *Fen* by Caryl Churchill in association with the Finborough Theatre and the National Theatre Studio. It became a sell out show and has been nominated for the Best Play Award in the London Awards for Art and Performance 2011.

We are pleased to be co-producing *Surfing Tommies* with BishBashBosh Productions and hope to continue our collaboration well into the future.

Co-Artistic Directors: John Hoggarth and Ria Parry
Company Associates: James Button, Paul Charlton, Claire Dargo, Neil Grainger, Kerry Irvine, Laura Keefe, David W Kidd, Racheli Sternberg, Elaine Yeung, BishBashBosh Productions

Iron Shoes, Limber View, Glasidale, Whitby, North Yorkshire YO21 2QU
ironshoesproductions@me.com
www.ironshoes.co.uk

Acknowledgements

I am indebted to the staff of the Museum of the Duke of Cornwall's Light Infantry, at Bodmin, Cornwall, for answering numerous questions about the regiment, and to Everard Wyrall's 1932 history of their involvement in the First World War. Tim Saunders kindly provided various pieces of Cornish for the play, and I am thankful for his advice. My continued thanks to Martin Baillie at BBC Radio Cornwall, and to the ongoing Cultural Events Programme of the United Nations Educational, Scientific and Cultural Organization World Heritage Site of the Cornwall and West Devon Mining Landscape. My considered thanks also to Professor Charles Thomas, and the Imperial War Museum, London. On death sentences passed by military courts of the British Army during this period, I am grateful for the scholarship of Gerard Oram and Julian Putkowski. The latter I would like to thank for his kind preface to this drama.

I would like to thank the following BishBashBosh Buddies for their continuing supoport:

J. Uttridge, M. Crome, E. Wooderson, Ruth Stock, G. Clarke, M. Roskrow, Pat Owen, Trevor Gardiner, Peter Pullen, Gail Ward, Tony McLennan, Zoe Hughes, Steve Endean, Wendy Woodcock, Tom Kennedy, Jimmy Carveth, Jamie Caruana, Robert Holland, Matthew Dearing, Mark and Jane Champion, Colin and Sylvia Honey, Gary Collins, Julia Dunstan, Gary Baker, Rhia Rogers and Derek Wills.

Alan M. Kent
May 2011

If you would like to become a Buddy, please contact
dean@bishbashboshproductions.co.uk

Preface

I know damn all about drama but I've studied a lot about the First World War, and enjoy sampling material that breaches the boundaries that confine our understanding of the conflict.

For me, 'Surfing Tommies' is a delicious confection, like well crafted crowst, but many military historians will find the play rather hard to swallow. No – it's not the surfing bit that will stick in their throats but the way in which Alan's imaginative drama subverts the established image of the Great War. The distinctive regional references, Cornish language, allusions to class conflict, fleshy joys and explicit criticism of military injustice, collectively undermine established dogma about a military cohesion.

The drama embraces and celebrates diversity, debate and change and doesn't rehash the conventional image of volunteers dutifully marching away to war. Instead of the musty 'Nation at Arms' we are treated to an intelligent, refreshing twenty-first century interpretation of the Great War, which includes acknowledgement of the conditional pardons granted in 2006 to soldiers who were executed 'for the sake of example'.

Such detail would have tickled the palate of Private George Mills, who served with the 2nd Battalion Duke of Cornwall's Light Infantry on the Western Front during 1915. Because he was a Cockney and worked as a docker in London's East End, 21-year-old George would have found the Cornish dialect a bit tough to digest at first and he didn't see much action in the trenches.

However, he was a bit of an amateur thespian, and when George decided to 'go home for a few days' he masqueraded as an officer and bounced a few cheques before being nabbed by military police. He disliked fighting, didn't smoke or drink and never surfed but he'd have had a melancholy understanding of John Pascoe's fate because George was the only soldier to be executed for attempting to desert from the Duke of Cornwall's Light Infantry.

Between speculation about an uneasy ghost hovering around the script and the rasping response of tetchy historians, 'Surfing Tommies' will provoke a range of reactions but few will miss the underlying message: we make history or it makes us.

Julian Putkowksi is a broadcaster and historian. He is the co-author of *Shot a Dawn: Executions in World War One by authority of the British Army Act*

The first production of *Surfing Tommies* was staged by BishBashBosh
Productions and performed in Cornwall in May and June 2009 with the
following performers:

Actor 1	Molly Weaver
Actor 2	Jamie Trotter
Actor 3	Trevor Cuthbertson
Actor 4	Ed Williams
Actor 5	Dean Nolan
Director	John Hoggarth
Associate director	Ria Parry
Stage Manager	Victoria Guy
Costuming	Pam Verran
Music	The People's String Foundation
Cornish language	Tim Saunders
Producer	Dean Nolan for BishBashBoshProductions
Playwright	Alan M. Kent

A note on the characters

Actor 1 – Female

Maisie Pascoe (b.1989) is completing a BA (Hons) in History at the Combined Universities of Cornwall, Tremough, Penryn, and is a surfing chick.

Rose Pascoe (1870–1960), former bal-maiden, now housewife and mother of John Henry Pascoe.

Mrs Slattery (1857–1927) works as a Senior at the offices of the *Western Daily Mercury*, Plymouth.

Michelle Méhauté (1890–1915), a Belgian prostitute.

Girl (1900–1980), a milk maid and the girlfriend of John Henry Pascoe.

Actor 2 – Male

John Henry Pascoe (1900–1915), only son of Rose Pascoe, and partner of Jimmy 'Dunkey' Tamblyn at North Wheal Leisure Mine, Perranporth.

Actor 3– Male

Cap'n William Tresawna (1869–1938), Day Cap'n at North Wheal Leisure Mine. Teetotaller and Methodist lay preacher.

Actor 4 – Male

Joseph Hocking (1860–1937), a minister of the United Methodist Free Churches and novelist.

Robert Walling (1890–1976), a journalist for the *Western Daily Mercury* and member of the Territorial army.

Commanding Officer (1890–1943), born Launceston, son of a banker. He had a career in finance before enlisting.

Christiaan van der Riet (1868–1919), South-African surfer, soldier and gold-miner, died of influenza in the epidemic of 1919.

Jack Polmassick (1883–1940), born at Bolingey, carpenter at North Wheal Leisure Mine. With his father, owner of Polmassick's funeral directors.

Actor 5 – Male

Jimmy 'Dunkey' Tamblyn (1888–1943), womaniser, pasty-eater, drunkard and donkey breeder, a tributer at North Wheal Leisure Mine.

Biographies

Molly Weaver – *Maisy Pascoe, Rose Pascoe, Mrs Slattery, Michelle Méhauté, Girl*

Molly began her training at the Hub Theatre School and went on to complete a degree in Contemporary Dance Choreography at Bath Spa University. Her first professional role was playing Mosca in Volpone and she went on to dance around the country, including at the opening of Jamie Oliver's restaurant Fifteen, and for the BBC's Blast projects, leading Cornwall for the BBC's Big Dance Guinness record attempt and choreographing for ITV's Doc Martin. Molly has toured nationally with C-Scape Dance Company on their Guilty Fingers tour, and with Rogue Theatre Company as Lolo the Clown in Madame Lucinda's Wonder Show. Molly joined BishBashBosh in 2008 and she has performed in *The Tin Violin*, *Surfing Tommies* and stage managed last year's show, *A Mere Interlude*. Molly has sung with several bands and now sings jazz with her act Molly the Moocha, playing Glastonbury Festival last year.

Toby Nicholas – *John Henry Pascoe*

Toby grew up in Whitsand Bay on the south east coast of Cornwall. He made his professional acting debut at the age of ten when he took on the role of Gavroche in Les Miserables and a year later played the title role in Lionel Bart's Oliver, both on Cameron Mackintosh's National Tours.

Growing up Toby was a typical country boy who loved being outdoors, especially surfing, and so moving to London in 2007 to train on Italia Conti's BA Acting Course was a big shock to the system. Although he has grown to love living in the capital, Toby is very excited to perform on home turf for his first theatre production since drama school and to share with the rest of the country this piece of Cornish history that he holds so close to his heart.

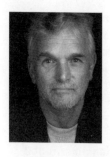

Trevor Cuthbertson – *Cap'n William Tresawna*
Trevor was born in Newcastle upon Tyne, and after dropping out of Salford University in 1974, has been based in Cornwall, where in 1998 he toured with John Godber's Bouncers. He has since studied at E15, where he won a freelance contract with the BBC RDC as part of the Carleton Hobbs Bursary Award scheme. He has appeared in several dramas for the BBC including Poirot, and The Gun Powder Plot. Other television and film work include Doc Martin and Explosions, which premiered at the Odeon Leicester Square as part of the 2006 London Film Festival. Recently he appeared as the child-processing butcher for Pindrop theatre's video Shine and on stage at the Headliners Comedy Club (Chiswick) as Squire Braggart in Richard O'Brien's Pig in Boots for the Wireless Theatre Company. Trevor appeared in the tour of *The Tin Violin* and the production of *Surfing Tommies* in 2009. Trevor spent last summer as a gentleman in the court of Henry VIII at Shakespeare's Globe whilst masquerading as the face of soft Swiss cheese.

Ed Williams – *Joseph Hocking, Robert Walling, Commanding Officer, Christiaan van der Riet, Jack Polmassick*
Ed trained at Royal Welsh College of Music and Drama, where productions included A Small Family Business and Macbeth. Since graduating, theatre credits include *Surfing Tommies* and *A Mere Interlude* (BishbashBosh), The Misanthrope (White Bear Theatre), Tribeca (Theatre 503) and The Taming Of The Shrew (Courtyard Theatre.) TV credits include Pleasure Park (ITV) and Hotel Babylon(BBC). Ed has also appeared in a number of short films including Peace Warriors, The Thin White Line and The Midway State. This is Ed's third outing with BishBashBosh.

Dean Nolan – *Jimmy 'Dunkey' Tamblyn*; *Producer*

Dean was born in Truro, Cornwall, and first trained at the Hub Theatre School in St Austell, where he toured with the show Volpone (playing Nano the Dwarf). He spent five years with the National Youth Theatre of Great Britain between 1999-2004 and performed in Nicholas Nickleby (Lyric Hammersmith; Lowry, Salford), Murder in the Cathedral (Southwark and Westminster cathedrals), Hanging Around (Watch this Space – National Theatre/Kneehigh collaboration) and The Master and Margarita (Lyric Hammersmith), becoming a company manager and workshop leader. Other work has included The Jungle Book (Warwick Arts Centre), Joseph and the Amazing Technicolor Dreamcoat (Bill Kenwright Ltd), Thomas and Friends Live (as the Fat Controller), Robin Hood and Babes in the Wood, A Taste of Honey, Romeo and Juliet Unzipped (Salisbury Playhouse) and Riot Rebellion and Bloody Insurrection, Sex, Docks and Rock n Roll (with Red Ladder Theatre and Chumbawamba). TV and film performances include Ashes to Ashes (BBC), Weekend Retreat (O-Region) and several commercials and short films. Dean has also performed in *Oogly Es Sin*, *Surfing Tommies* and *A Mere Interlude* for BishBashBosh, where he is co-artistic director.

John Hoggarth – *Director*

John Hoggarth was born and brought up in Whitby, North Yorkshire. He trained and worked as an actor for several years before expanding his work to include writing and directing. In recent years he has combined the artistic directorship of the National Youth Theatre with a prolific writing career. He has had his work produced for television, radio and the stage. John has also developed a reputation for developing burgeoning comedy talent and has seen recent collaborations led to a Perrier nomination, and the winning of both So Think You're Funny? and the BBC new talent award. In 2008 John married Ria Parry and together they run IRON SHOES, an independent theatre company promoting creative talent and supporting emerging writers. Iron Shoes' production of Crush won a Fringe First at the 2009 Edinburgh Fringe Festival. In 2010 John co-wrote and directed the sketch show The Ginge, The

Geordie and The Geek which had a total sell-out run of the festival, the same team return to the 2011 festival with two separate shows each full of fun and laughter. Productions as director include: Oramix, (2011), The Kerryman (2010), The Ginge The Geordie and The Geek (Edinburgh Festival 2010), The Comedy Bitch (Edinburgh Festival, 2010); A Mere Interlude (Minack Theatre, Cornwall 2010); Howl (The Lyric Theatre, Belfast 2009); Fastburn, (Kneehigh Theatre 2009); Surfing Tommies (South-West Tour 2009); The Tin Violin (Cornwall Tour 2008); Whose Shoes? NYT/Lowry Theatre; Much Ado About Nothing (NYT/Hackney Empire); Still Killing Time (NYT/Soho Theatre); Citizenship (NYT/National Theatre); Master and Margarita (NYT/Lyric Hammersmith); Kes (NYT/Lyric Hammersmith); The Dutch Elm Conservatoire (Pleasance Edinburgh); Tailor Made Love (Theatre 503); Amadeus (Belfast and all Ireland tour, Gauntlet Theatre Company). John is currently working with the Young Vic in London and developing several scripts for Iron Shoes. John has written numerous plays and dramas for the television, radio and the stage. Recent scripts that have gone into production include: The Water Still Remains (Lowry Centre, Salford), Crossing The Line (Short film for The Premiership), Fastburn, (NYT/Kneehigh Theatre Company.) A Salford Macbeth, (Lowry Theatre); Two series of The Correspondent written as commission for BBC7 and now broadcast on BBC Radio 4; i-pod do you? Soho Theatre; Tom Allen and other Short Stories, The Gilded Balloon Edinburgh; Watch Over Me I-IV (Four series of a teenage soap opera initially commissioned by the parents of murdered school girl Milly Dowler); Whose Shoes? Lowry Theatre/NYT.

Ria Parry – Associate Director

Ria is Co-Artistic Director of Iron Shoes. She received the Leverhulme Directors' Bursary in 2010–2011, becoming Director in Residence at the National Theatre Studio and directing Fen by Caryl Churchill at the Finborough Theatre. Ria won a Fringe First Award for Crush by Paul Charlton at the Edinburgh Festival. The production was shortlisted for the Carol Tambor New York Award and received two Stage Award nominations, before completing a national tour. Other directing includes Mad about the Boy by Gbolahan Obisesan (West Yorkshire Playhouse), Catch by Emma Jowett (Lost Theatre, New Writing Award),

Rewind and King Lear (Young Vic). For Box Clever Theatre, she has directed tours of The Hate Play, The Tempest and The Buzz. Ria was a Creative Producer at Watford Palace Theatre for two years. She studied at Royal Holloway University and on the National Theatre Studio Director's Course.

The People's String Foundation – *Music*
Cornwall is the appropriate home for the beautifully evocative, languid and lush music of The People's String Foundation. Theirs is unfamiliar territory, scaling the heights of jazz, hip-hop beat-work, Middle Eastern melodies – performed with an eye toward experimentation and nods toward the avant-garde. Essentially the brainchild of multi-instrumentalist and jazz singer Ben Sutcliffe and world/blues guitarist Zaid Al-Rabiki, the duo combine to wonderful songwriting effect but it's in their live performances that the group's powerful dynamics come to the fore, the duo enlisting the assistance of a troupe of inspired and talented musicians.

Stephen Robinson – *Company Stage Manager*
Stephen joins the Bish Bash Bosh team for the first time as Company Stage Manager having recently worked with Spike Theatre on their productions, On Top of the World and The Olympics, Fools Proof Theatre's Je Suis Dead, Milan Govedarica's production of Me As A Pengui and various community arts projects with Zho Productions and Tuebrook Transnational. His passion for film has seen him join Blue Monkey Productions as an artistic producer on their recent horror film, Leashed, and as an actor/performer with Artemis Productions, an international street theatre company that he co-founded in 2001. Stephen lists amongst his interests, '...breaking and fixing things' a skill he hopes not to apply to the actors on this tour.

Pam Verran– *Costume designer*

Pam works as a freelance costume designer with a background as a costume maker. She studied textiles at Cornwall College and costume interpretation for the performing arts at the London College of Fashion. Her theatre work includes Mind The Gap by Shallal Dance Theatre Company, The Magic Flute and Hamlet by Cube Theatre, Hyde and Seek by Zenith Theatre; her film work includes Alice in Wonderland directed by Tim Burton, Treasure Island directed by Hansjurg Thurn and Apocalypto directed by Mel Gibson and Keeping Mum directed by Niall Johnson. For television she has worked on Mcfly, The Three Daft Monkeys and Rosie and The Goldbugs. She recently returned to the BBC in Birmingham as wardrobe mistress on Doctors. Her specialist area is corsetry and Victorian costume.

Jane Verity – *Press Officer*

Jane grew up in Armley, Leeds. She studied English Literature at Durham University and worked for three years as press officer at West Yorkshire Playhouse. She is currently completing an MA in Creative Writing at the University of Manchester, is press officer at Red Ladder Theatre Company and is working on freelance PR projects. In between straddling the worlds of creative writing and arts PR, she runs a gymnastics club, where she teaches people to straddle other things; mostly vaults.

Rebecca Hunt – *BishBashBosh support*

Rebecca is studying A levels at Cornwall College and a subsidiary diploma in acting. She became involved with BishBashBosh after seeing a performance of *Surfing Tommies* at Penrice Community College. Rebecca hopes to go to drama school and become an actress.

Maddy Murray – *BishBashBosh support*

Maddy fell in love with BishBashBosh last year when she went to see their performance of *A Mere Interlude*. She really enjoys working with the company and hopes to go to drama school on completing her A levels at Truro College.

Alan M. Kent – *Playwright*

Alan M. Kent was born in St Austell, Cornwall, and studied at the Universities of Cardiff and Exeter. He is a Lecturer in Literature for the Open University in South-West Britain, and a Visiting Lecturer in Celtic Literature at the University of A Coruña, Galicia. A prize-winning poet, novelist and dramatist, he has written extensively on Cornwall and Celtic Studies. In 1998, he won the Charles Lee Literary Prize, in 1999 a Euroscript Award, in 2004 Joint Winner of the Holyer an Gof Literary Salver, and in 2007 and 2008, winner of the Cornish Gorsedd Poetry in English Prize. He is the author of *The Literature of Cornwall: Continuity, Identity, Difference 1000–2000* (2000) and *Ordinalia: The Cornish Mystery Play Cycle – A Verse Translation* (2005). He co-edited *Looking at the Mermaid: A Reader in Cornish Literature 800–1900* (2000) and *The Busy Earth: A Reader in Global Cornish Literature 1700–2000* (2008). Other recent publications include *Cousin Jack's Mouth-Organ: Travels in Cornish America* (2004), *Proper Job, Charlie Curnow!* (2005), *Stannary Parliament* (2006), *Electric Pastyland* (2007), *Druid Offsetting* (2008) and *Voodoo Pilchard* (2010). Recent drama includes *Nativitas Christi* (2006), *Oogly es Sin* (2007), *The Tin Violin* (2008) and *A Mere Interlude* (2010). His latest academic work is *The Theatre of Cornwall: Space, Place, Performance* (2010). He is the editor of *Four Modern Cornish Plays* (2010) and co-editor of *The Francis Boutle Book of Cornish Short Stories*. His collection of poetry *The Hope of Place: Selected Poems in English 1990–2010* was also published to critical acclaim in 2010.

Top left: John Hoggarth (*left*) and Trevor Cuthbertson reading through the script
Top right: Molly Weaver
Bottom, left to right: Ria Parry, Dean Nolan, John Hoggarth with a load of biscuits

From the 2009 tour of Surfing Tommies: top Jimmy Tamblyn (Dean Nolan) and Cap'n William
Tresawna (Trevor Cuthbertson)
Bottom: Jimmy Tamblyn and Robert Walling (Ed Williams)

From the 2009 tour of Surfing Tommies Michelle Méhauté (Molly Weaver)

Top: Girl (Molly Weaver) and Jimmy Tamblyn (Dean Nolan)
Bottom: Jimmy Tamblyn, Robert Walling (Ed Williams) and Cap'n Tresawna (Trevor Cuthberton) going surfing.

A note on the text

This play is a drama, and is therefore invention. However, the story of the return of Cornishmen from the First World War to begin surfing is well known. According to many observers they were taught by South African soldiers who fought with them in the conflict.

Three of the characters in the play are based on real people:

ROBERT WALLING (1890–1976), was born in Plymouth, educated at Plymouth College, and worked as a journalist for the *Western Daily Mercury*. He was a member of the Territorial army, working with both the Royal Garrison Artillery and, later, the Tank Corps. He lived in Plympton and London. One of his achievements was to produce the magazine *An Howlsedhas/The West*, one of the less well-known artefacts of the Cornish language revival. Three copies of this remarkable magazine survive.

The play mentions Walling corresponding with HENRY JENNER. Jenner (1848–1934) was born at St Columb Major, Cornwall, and in the course of a long career at the British Museum in London discovered a number of works of Cornish literature, as well as becoming increasingly aware of the surviving oral traditions in west Cornwall. Jenner completed in 1904 *A Handbook of the Cornish Language*, which not only gave a history of the Cornish language, but offered elementary study of vocabulary and grammar. In his *Handbook*, Jenner famously asked 'Why should Cornishmen learn Cornish? ... The question is a fair one, the answer is simple. Because they are Cornishmen.' Walling was obviously interested in Jenner's book and influenced by his written form of Cornish.

The REVEREND JOSEPH HOCKING (1860–1937) was born in St Stephen-in-Brannel, and was a minister of the United Methodist Free Churches. During the late nineteenth and early twentieth century, he was a best-selling novelist, establishing the genre of the historical-romantic novel. During the First World War, as well as writing a number of War-themed novels, Hocking also became a leading army recruitment worker. Although initially distant from the Cornish Revival of the early twentieth-century, Hocking later embraced its values. He lived for a while at Perranporth.

To this day, Perranporth, not only remains a centre of surfing, but also of Cornish identity. Every year, a parade and drama re-enact the life of Cornwall's 'first surfer' – St Piran – on the closest Sunday to St Piran's Day (5th March).

Surfing Tommies

Act One

1. Abandoned North Wheal Leisure Mine, Perranporth, Cornwall, at the start of the twenty-first century.
2. A shaft, North Wheal Leisure Mine, Perranporth, Cornwall, 30 June, 1914.
3. Later: The exterior of North Wheal Leisure Mine, 30 June, 1914.
4. The exterior of the North Wheal Leisure Mine, 2 July, 1914.
5. The 'Western Daily Mercury' newspaper office, Plymouth, 2 July, 1914.
6. The kitchen of the Pascoe household, Pencrennow Farm, 7 July, 1914.
7. The sand dunes, Perranporth, 10 July, 1914.
8. Tywarnhayle Square, Perranporth, 15 July, 1914.
9. Shaft No. 6 at North Wheal Leisure Mine, Perranporth, 12 August, 1914.
10. The Duke of Cornwall Light Infantry depot, Bodmin, 15 September, 1914.

Act Two

1. A Communications Trench, near the Somme, 3 July, 1915.
2. Abandoned North Wheal Leisure Mine, Perranporth, Cornwall, at the start of the twenty-first century.
3. Excavation tunnel and trench at Mons, 12 November, 1914.
4. The kitchen of the Pascoe household, Pencrennow Farm, 12 November, 1914.
5. A trench system, Flanders, near Ypres, 5 January, 1915.
6. The streets of St Omer, 14 February, 1915.
7. A front-line trench, near the Second Battle of Ypres, 22 April, 1915
8. A Trench System, near the Somme, 29 June, 1915.
9. A Trench System, near the Somme, 1 July, 1915.
10. A Communications Trench, near the Somme, 3 July, 1915

Act Three
1. Abandoned North Wheal Leisure Mine, Perranporth, Cornwall, at the start of the twenty-first century.
2. A shaft, North Wheal Leisure Mine, Perranporth, Cornwall, 31 July, 1918.
3. The kitchen of the Pascoe household, Pencrennow Farm, 7 August, 1918.
4. Polmassick's funeral directors and carpentery workshop, Perranporth, 20 September, 1918.
5. Shaft No. 6 at North Wheal Leisure Mine, Perranporth, 12 October, 1918.
6. The 'Western Daily Mercury' newspaper office, Plymouth 8 November, 1918.
7. Perran Sands, facing the Atlantic Ocean, 10 November, 1918.
8. Tywarnhayle Square, Perranporth, 10 November, 1918.
9. Perranporth Beach, 11 November, 1918.
10. The Atlantic Ocean, 11 November, 1918.

Act One

1. Abandoned North Wheal Leisure Mine, Perranporth, Cornwall, at the start of the twenty-first century.

The World Heritage Site remnants of North Wheal Leisure Mine, Perranporth. Positioned stage right is a horizontal shaft, made of A-framed grimy timber and rusty corrugated iron. The shaft runs into a dark distance, and from it, appear the tracks of a tram-road, once used by the miners for tramming. The shaft is sealed with an iron grid, and around it are pieces of random, rusty mining paraphernalia. One of the important items left is a rusty sticking tommy (a twist of metal forming a candle-holder to wedge into rock or wood). The overall look should be of neglect and wear, but as the play continues, it gradually becomes re-activated.

Centre-stage rear is a tarpaulined screen (for projections), while on stage-left, rear, are some vertical pieces of rusty, corrugated iron. These curve over at the top and will double as the trenches later on. Beneath them are duck-boards. One sign reads 'Danger: Blasting'. Another has 'Bad Air: Keep Out'. Downstage left are a table and chairs, which will double for various locations in the play. These are in the period style of the early twentieth century. Stage left a single door and frame, with a frosted glass window. We hear the sounds of drilling, picks, gads, shovels, and men's voices. These quieten and merge into the sound of waves crashing upon a shore. This matches a projection of barrelling waves breaking. Hear the swash of water through pebbles and stones. In the style of a passionate Methodist minister, a VOICEOVER *reads Psalm 107: 23-26.*

VOICEOVER: They that go down to the sea in ships that do business in great waters: These see the works of the Lord, and his wonders in the deep. For he commandeth, and raiseth the stormy wind, which lifteth up the waves thereof. They mount up to the heavens, they go down to the depths: their soul is melted because of trouble.

The VOICEOVER *merges into the song: 'Hail to the Homeland'. This fuses into a piece of trance/euphoria-style rave music, with a centre-stage rear laser, gradually rising upwards, and illuminating a female figure carrying a surf-board under her arm. The euphoric trance music rises to a climax. The figure is* MAISIE PASCOE. *She is wearing a 'Gul' one-piece neoprene wetsuit; her hair wet from the Atlantic Ocean. The board is wet and sandy, as is her wetsuit.*

MAISIE: You a'right? I saw you earlier. I always take this short cut see, past North Wheal Leisure. Yeah ... No rip-off parking charges. Not many people knaw about ut. All filled in now – this was where the main shaft was, years ago, like. It was a'right this mornin' wudn' it? Radio said it'd be clean. Perfect a-frames off the Atlantic ... So I'm doin' these cut backs an' a floater, an' it's all goin' well. The last half an hour was useless – all blown out. I stick to Penhale. Near the town, well, thaas where all the muppets and groms are. You knaw the type: got a Quicksilver or Billabong hoodie an' they think their God's gift. Fakies an' total frubes who 'ent got a clue. Kooks mullerin' out after five seconds right? I'm down there this mornin', right, just past Perran Beach an' there's this Ripcurl-clad knobber lookin' like ee's somethun outta' Baywatch runnin' down – new long board on him like, not a mark on it. You gotta' laugh. An' ee's posin' to all us lot right ... me and me mates are laughin' coz he thinks 'ee's so cool. So, he asks me my name, and I tell him it's Maisie, Maisie Pascoe. "Nice name," 'ee says. "Unusual." Then 'ee's all "you should have been here yesterday", so I says to him "I was", and the day before that, an' the day before that one, an' the week before, an' the year before. "I was surfing before I was walking, see," I goes to him. I tell him the sea's in my soul. Part of me. Deep inside. Then he walks off, with a real attitude on un. I see un later and 'ee's like, "Can I text ya?" And I'm like "Na, you're okay". So then he's on about his Facebook site an' tha'. So "Okay," I says. I might look him up... But I'm only flirtin' right? I'm not interested. You know how it is. What they dun't realise, is that it's all beyond 'Run to the Sun' right? Oh yeah – you see 'em dun'cha' comin' down the A30 in their VW campers that daddy's bought them – yeah – split-screen collectable jobs like – and they turn up like they own the place. So after a few rides, it's then up to Newquay, yeah? You know the score. Start over Berties, then Central, maybe go back Sailors, then down Walkabout, clubbing all night – you know, a bit of Ministry of Sound, some Chilis, bit of drum 'n' bass to round it off –

'til you end up groping some sweaty emmet on the dance-floor t'some crap like Celine Dion, then falling fur some romantic walk on Towan before they try to cop off with you ... Been there, seen it, got the t-shirt, yeah. It's worse this time ov year though – when the Unis an' schools all kick out...

As MAISIE *speaks, from the rear of the stage,* JOHN HENRY PASCOE *enters, wearing the mining fatigues he has on for the remainder of Act One, but no helmet. He is obviously a figure from another age. He stands austerely watching her, gazing into the audience, but as Maisie continues speaking, he smiles, becoming more animated, eventually moving to gracefully mime surfing. His shadow should be high-lighted on the screen.*

MAISIE: So I'm at uni too right? I mean I had the option of goin' away, but I'm doing history down Tremough. I thought, well, what's the point? Yeah, Cornwall can suck big-time but it's got its good points too. So I'm into me history like ... Thaas why I come up here. There's a lot of history up Wheal Leisure. More than that though ... There's like a presence ... Ghosts, I s'pose. You feel them in the shafts and the adits ... watchin' ... We do barbecues up here in the summer. I mean we 'ent supposed to now, like because the Council got money to do all these places up, yeah ... Objective One funding. All European money. You still find stuff though. Some ov ut 'ent been moved in years. They say North Wheal Leisure closed overnight. Price ov tin dropped after the First World War, an' that was ut. The men expected t'be back at work the following week. Never happened. When the war ended, there was no need for any tin. They say if you go inside you'll find ut just like 'twas left. Some chance of that now. See...

MAISIE *rattles the cap grid. It doesn't move.*

MAISIE: Good job we've got surfin' now or we'd have nothun' ... I mean see they crowd down Crofty. How long ago wuz ut that that shut, and some party went in t'try t'open ut up again? They still 'ent even raised a ton ov tin. Here though, you'n still find ut. I mean look at this stuff...

MAISIE *notices a rusted sticking tommy. She picks it up. As she does so, the figure of* JOHN HENRY PASCOE *stops surfing and looks at her. He holds a sticking tommy too – and as Maisie holds and turns it, holding it up to the light, this is echoed in his movements.*

MAISIE: This look. A sticking tommy. They make them now for tourists

3

over Mount Pleasant Eco-Park. Used them to see with, back years ago ... A light in the dark. Comforting like, in all that blackness underground. Not much good fur anything now...

MAISIE *drops the sticking tommy. It clatters to the floor. At this,* JOHN HENRY PASCOE *leaves the stage.*

MAISIE: Right, I best be gettin' back. Conditioner on the hair. Get me straighteners out. There's a band on down the Watering Hole tonight ... My mate's in it ... Be filled with emmets I 'spect, reckonin' they're livin' the dream. Supping on Doom Bar, an' gettin out their heads on blow outside ... Wanna' come? Can if you want...

MAISIE *turns, obviously chilled at a presence.*

MAISIE: Sorry ... for a moment, I thought there was someone there ... It must be ... must be ... the rip off the Atlantic ... Then, thaas Cornwall fur 'ee. Always more full ov the past than the future. Right, I'm off home fur a shower an' t'get changed. Laters ... Might even text that emmet fur a laugh...

The euphoria music merges into 'Hail to the Homeland'.

2. A shaft, North Wheal Leisure Mine, Perranporth, Cornwall, 30 June, 1914.

Two figures enter from out of the shaft, both of them coughing and spluttering. Both are tin miners, wearing hats and runs of candles around their necks. One of them is JOHN HENRY PASCOE. *The other is tributer* JIMMY 'DUNKEY' TAMBLYN. JOHN HENRY *is slight and a young man; while* JIMMY *is a man-mountain.* JIMMY *has a thick moustache. From inside the shaft we hear their voices. Music fades.*

JIMMY: [*shouting back*] Comest thou on John Henry ... We'm near the end ... I was right, see ... 'Es, I remember this run down ... I d'knaw North Wheal Leisure like the back of me hand ... leastways when I'n see ut...

JOHN HENRY: I am ... 'Tis dark though ... an' I keep catchin' me feet on the sleepers of the tarnin' trammels...

JIMMY: Keep on goin' ... I knaw 'tis tight ... The durns is some low you ... Argh ... [*banging his head on one of the durns*] What a fuggan piece of floor fustin flew this be!

JOHN HENRY: I'm almost there...

JIMMY *steps out covered in tin dust. After brushing off his clothes, he sits on a piece of industrial debris and touches pipe. Then he takes off his helmet and rubs his head.*

JIMMY: [*peering into the audience*] Caw d'hell. 'Tis near darker out here than 'twas in there. [*exasperated*] Giss' on with 'ee...

JOHN HENRY *steps out into the light, and dusts himself down.*

JOHN HENRY: I'm lampered up a bewdie.

JIMMY: We'm properly buggered now pard an' naw mistake...

JOHN HENRY: What 'ee mean Jimmy? Wozon?

JIMMY: Well, that there dunkey ov a dab hand, Boy Polmassick, 'ave made the durns of the drang here too low. The dropper should be least seven foot, and 'ee idn' nowhere near tha' fur certain ... 'Ee'll wish 'is cake cough when Tresawna'll catch up widn'. You'll see ... You knaw what Tresawna be like. If tidn' dun right, 'twill be dun right by end of core. I'n hear un already: [*in posh, bass accent*] "Tamblyn, why in 'eaven's name 'ebm you set those durns right? I dun't pay 'ee t'mark time. Mark time in your own time if you must." "Well, Cap'n Tresawna ... 'Tis like this ..." I'll put un straight. "You d'need t'have a yap with Polmassick, over carpenter's shop. Ever since that there g'eat lump ov elvan fell on 'un back on the 90 fathom level, honest t'God, 'ee 'edn been 'zactly right in the head..."

JOHN HENRY: I thought 'ee knew what 'ee was doin' ov.

JIMMY: Knaw what 'ee wuz doin' ov? Knaw what 'ee wuz doin ov! This is Cornish hard-rock mining. Nobody d'knaw what they'm doin' ov ... 'Tis ninety-nine per cent guess work and one per cent luck. Boy, there's a helleva' lot you still gotta' learn 'bout minin '... 'Tidn just digging stuff out the ground ... oh no ... thaas the easy part. You got t' knaw tin, see ... Thaas me, see. I d' knaw tin ...[*sniffs like a connoisseur*] I'n smell ut. I got the noase fur ut. 'Tis in me blood. In me veins.

JOHN HENRY: You say tha', but we 'ebm 'ad a spurt for what ... near on a month now...

JIMMY: Yeah ... you'm right there. We'm bit wisht at the moment, but dun't 'ee worry. 'Twill pick up 'gain. Always does. An' you, John Henry Pascoe, is workin' with the very best ... James 'Dunkey' Tamblyn ... I've made more tonnage in this parish than any man ...

'Ere boy – 'ave us over that sticking tommy will 'ee? I cen't see bugger all here.

JOHN HENRY *searches around for a sticking tommy.*

JIMMY: Light un up boy...

JOHN HENRY *strikes a match, takes a candle, lights it and places it in the metal holder, then jams it into the timbering. The glow lights the shuttering timbers.*

JIMMY: Thaas better. Now we'n see what we'n doin' ov. Time fur a bit ov crowst, I reckon.

JOHN HENRY: Crowst? But we 'ebm been at ut more than an hour...

JIMMY: An' my belly d'already think me throawt been cut.

From his pasty pail JOHN HENRY *takes out an average-sized pasty.*

JIMMY: Hold the crimping mind boy. This place be full a' arsenic...

JIMMY *reaches in his crib bag for his own pasty, which is enormous. The two compare sizes.*

JOHN HENRY: [*laughing*] Who made 'ee tha'?

JIMMY: A maid I d'knaw back Bolingey. A big girl true 'nough. Good on a turnip though. An' not bad on carrot neether. She d'knaw 'ow t'keep a man happy.

JOHN HENRY: [*joking*] Size idn' everything tho' es ut Mr Tamblyn?

JIMMY: Get away with 'ee. Course 'tis ... Some'un like this'll keep 'ee goin' all morning – sturt ov tin, or naw sturt of tin. Mark my words ... when you'm settled down, first thing you'll want t'make sure ov is that the maid can put teddy, turnip an' onion t'pastry. She'n be purty as y'like but if she can't make 'ee a decent oggie then 'tidn' worth ut, my son [*sniffs*].

JIMMY *pulls out a newspaper – a copy of the 'Western Daily Mercury'.* JIMMY *puts his feet up, as if settling in for the full morning.*

JOHN HENRY: We staying here all morning? Wun't Cap'n be long in a minute? I heard tell 'ee be shawing someone 'round today.

JIMMY: So what if 'ee is. I dun't take orders from Tresawna ... 'Ee idn' no more than you or me, but with a bowler hat and waistcut on bought-

6

en down Trura. 'Ee d'make me laugh: 'ee d'speak all cut up when the shareholders is all 'round, but when 'tis you an' me, 'ee be some broad. Gaa – 'ee's always graffled up like an arish pig with 'is nawse in the air ... 'Ee be no more fit fur mining than a stocking do be on a man's nose. I tell 'ee, 'ee d'swear an 'ole in an iron pot if 'ee 'ad the chance.

JOHN HENRY: I gotta' take notice ov un though ... 'ee knawin' mother an' all...

JIMMY: Well, yes ... You'n be polite an' that. I mean, I knaw 'ee got 'ee the job an tha', but that dun't mean you gotta' stand to attention every time 'ee d'speak. Tresawna d'knaw about as much about minin' as I knaw how to fart like a steer ... an' that idn' very much. Besides tha', 'ee's too much of a Methodee fur my likin' ... When a miner dun't take a drop ov drink down the Wink, well, 'tis come to someun'. Dunnee' worry 'bout 'ee. There's bigger things to worry about in the world – least, by the look ov ut 'ere...

JIMMY *stabs the front page of the newspaper with his forefinger.*

JOHN HENRY: What 'ee mean?

JIMMY: Have a gake. You've 'eard 'ebm 'ee? All that there goin' on over in Sarajev-ee-o ... Some bugger have been an' shot the Archduke of Austria ... Crowd by the name ov the Black Hand Group. 'Ere, look. [*points to the story*] 'Twill all fall now like a proper set ov cards topplin' ... I tell 'ee straight ... Our crowd'll be in there next...

JOHN HENRY: That wun't affect we will ut? We'm miles from all that ben't us?

JIMMY: Well, that wun't the way 'twas down South Africee. When it all blawed up on the Rand, thousands of us Cornish wuz affected ... Stupid buggers cudn' sort 'ut out ... Faather wuz out there then. Made a fair old mint in the goldfields. Mind you, lost moast ut gamblin' back Johannesburg. Mother wun' too happy ... She give un jip when 'ee got back hoam after a year an' a half away with a couple ov crown in 'is pocket.

JOHN HENRY *steps forward to audience.* JIMMY *continues reading the newspaper, every so often shaking his head.*

JOHN HENRY: So, you can see how 'tis by now. I'm with Tamblyn 'ere. A good man really. But he likes a drop of ale. Has what 'ee calls 'is 'Coming-Off-Shift-Special', or three, or four, or twelve. 'Ee's never home. Always down the pub or the Wink. And women ... well, I dunno how 'ee d'do ut. I mean, 'ee be more ov a bear than a man. 'Ee d'go through three or four a week, 'less 'ee got um on rotation. Works hard though. Mother sorted it fur me, fur when I left school. When I turned fifteen. See, she'd always known Cap'n Tresawna. Well, she'd knawn ov un from Chapel. He's a stickler like, fur all that. Preachin' on a Sunday. 'Ee d'like all the miners an' families t'go. So 'twas all, "When might the lad be ready fur the mine then Mrs Pasca?" "Well, he d'leave school next month Mr Tresawna. 'Ee'll be there fur 'ee then..." "Thaas good, Mrs Pasca ... because we'm takin' on a few boys right now..." So thaas how I'm 'ere with Tamblyn. Simple as y'like. And thaas me I was always destined fur the mine. Just like faather wuz...

JIMMY *moves to be parallel with* JOHN HENRY.

JIMMY: So, you can see how 'tis by now. I got this lad with me. All set up by Tresawna. Ol' boy's mother idn' a bad-looking maid, an' she got brass and front enough t' make a copper kettle. Good ol' boy really – but a bit green behind the ears. Got hands like a maid still. Moaning on this week about the blisters on his fingers. We'll soon sort that out. 'Ee gotta' be trained up a bit fust. Well, t'begin with, 'ee dunno is ass from an adit underground. 'Bout the moast 'ee can do is shovel a bit ov stent. But ol' boy's comin on I s'pause. Wun't be bad once 'ee've grown up a bit. I d'tease 'im a bit, see. I d'say, "Johnny Pascoe, 'ebm you got no maid yet – to be goin' courtin' up on the downs?" "I don't go in fur much of tha'," says 'ee t'me. "You will do boy," says I. "Wait an' see". Thaas me tonight. I got a little romantic rendezvous down village all lined up ... Never mind all that goin' on over Austria, I say make hay when the sun shines ... Hey ... come on John Henry ... I be clemmed t' the marra with cold. Let's make 'iss back up the run...

JOHN HENRY: 'Ere Mr Tamblyn ... Shall us see Polmassick 'bout the durns?

JIMMY: We shall. Tresawna'll be long in a minute too. You'm right. 'Twun't do if we'm sprouncing round here...

JOHN HENRY *and* JIMMY *head back up the shaft.*

3. Later: The exterior of North Wheal Leisure Mine, 30 June, 1914.

Enter Cap'n William Tresawna, with his thumbs tucked into his waistcoat, proudly showing off the mining machinery. He is talking to Robert Walling, journalist for the 'Western Daily Mercury', who is writing notes in a leather-bound short-hand book.

WILLIAM: So you see, Mr ... a ....

WALLING: Walling...

WILLIAM: So you see, Mr Walling, North Wheal Leisure is the very pinnacle of the modern tin-mining facility. Each level, each fathom, is dug with the kind of precision our forefathers never knew, thanks to technology, and of course, faith in the good Lord above. There is never guess-work in the industry these days. No wonder there were so many accidents years ago. Do you know, we've not had a single incident here for three years now? Our safety record is exemplary.

WALLING: And so to confirm ... for my article, the erection of the new head-frame over the engine shaft will be completed by next week?

WILLIAM: By Friday, at the latest.

WALLING: Good. And we've done everything? Let me just check my notes: survey office, blacksmith's shop, spalling shed, compressor house and the new boiler house...

WILLIAM: There's only the miner's dry and the count house ... but I can show you those on the way back.

WALLING: I see ... And may I ask you one more important question Cap'n Tresawna, do you see a future for tin mining in Cornwall? There are, as you know, lots of voices who say the great age is over.

WILLIAM: Of course I do. I see no reason why we will not be carrying on mining here for the next thousand years. Especially with the new rock drills we have invested in. And that dust-laying spray is a godsend. Our newly-signed contract with Nobel's Explosives Company is also indicative of a bright future. And the new tramming on the 40 fathom level ... Make sure you mention that ... if you will...

WALLING: I will, of course, but tell me, what about the war? My editor will want some comment on this ... There is already news of coal miners enlisting in the north. Will the same thing occur in Cornwall?

WILLIAM: What of it? The war is distant from us. I can't see it affecting things too much here. I mean, the war should prompt requests for more tin, not less. Even if I'm called up, someone will carry it on...

WALLING: I'm keen to get out there if I can. I've signed up. My editor has me lined up as a special correspondent. Should be over quite quickly ... A glorious victory, I think.

WILLIAM: No war's a glorious victory, Mr Walling ... but preparation is all, so they say.

WALLING: Listen Cap'n Tresawna, I will need a word or two with some of the miners if that's alright. Just to hear their side of it, you see ... Have you someone you might recommend?

JIMMY 'DUNKEY' TAMBLYN *steps backwards out of the shaft, loudly and badly singing 'Little Lize' to himself.*

JIMMY: [*along the shaft*] An' she said:

'Little Lize I love you, honey,
Little Lize I love you (honey)
Little Lize I love you,
I love you in the springtime and the fall...

Go on boy ... thread un through, thaas it ... We'll be off down bottoms to do the same again in a minute...

WALLING: Perhaps this man...

WILLIAM: Well, he wouldn't be my first choice ... He's Tamblyn ... a bit cack-handed if you knaw what I mean ... Not very reliable ... Drinks a bit ... Breeds dunkey ... Dun't ever go chapel.

WALLING: Excuse me ... Might I have a word?

JIMMY: Morning sir ... Mornin Cap'n Tresawna ... The boy an' I are just workin' on that ladder road you asked us to put in ... Some tin up there, you ... Good stuff as well...

WILLIAM: This is Mr Walling. A journalist from the Western Daily Mercury.

JIMMY: [*excited*] The Mercury? Really? [*shouting in*] Hear that Johnny. The Mercury's here an' they want t'talk to Jimmy Tamblyn. Put it there Mr Walling. Jimmy Tamblyn, mining legend. You've probably heard ov me. Moast people 'ave.

JIMMY *vigorously shakes the hand of* WALLING.

WALLING: I've spoken to Captain Tresawna, and he's told me all about the new investment here. An exemplar of how mining should be completed these days? What's your understanding, Mr Tamblyn?

JIMMY *puts his hand around the shoulder of walling, and leads him away from* WILLIAM.

JIMMY: [*with a sharp intake of breath*] Do you want my most honestest response to tha'?

WALLING: [*slow*] Please ... it can be strictly between us two...

JIMMY: [*fast*] Complete waste ov bleddy time an' money ... and you'n most certainly put that in the paper if y'like.

WALLING: But...

JIMMY: You'n put as much equipment an' investment down a mine as you want, but if you 'ebm got boys like me and Tear-on Trewaves, Piff-widden Polgaver, and Doan't Naw Nothin' Northey, you 'ebm got a 'ope in 'ell. Tell 'ee truth, you may as well not bother...

WALLING: Is that true?

JIMMY: 'Course 'tis true. That old Billy goat Tresawna think 'ee d'knaw everything. His answer t'everything is more technology, more speed, more yield. That idn' how it d'work, my son. You want the real side of this, meet me down the pub after shift and I'll put 'ee straight ... What 'ee like? Brown ale or stout ... I'll take a pint ov Spingo, if you'm buy-in'...

WILLIAM *comes over.*

WILLIAM: I hope Mr Tamblyn is presenting our good side to you, Mr Walling.

WALLING: Well ... I certainly am seeing a different side...

JIMMY: [*interrupting*] 'Course I am Cap'n. You d'knaw I would never let you down ... Always positive, me ... And as I wuz saying, these new investments are totally supported by the boys...

JIMMY *winks at* WALLING.

WALLING: So what's your thoughts, Mr Tamblyn?

JIMMY: My thoughts ... 'zactly ... upon wha' 'zactly?

WALLING: On mining. On Cornwall.

JIMMY: Well, we Cornish are a bit special like. A bit mazed in the head. An rugby mad. An good wrasslers. An' when you've got such amazin' leaders ov industry as Mr Tresawna here ... there's nothun' to worry 'bout.

WALLING: There are moves, you know, suggested by contributors to the Cornish Magazine who say Cornwall should give up its industry ... Look to its history and language for a way forward ... Idlers and day-trippers too...

JIMMY: 'Es ... I've 'eard all 'bout that – but dunnee' take much notice ... 'Tidn like we'm all goin' t'start speakin' Cornish again is ut? And trippers ... now why should they want t'be heading down here? There idn' nothun' here but a pile ov rocks ... In fact, thaas Cornwall all over 'ent ut – just an interestun' pile ov rocks...

WILLIAM: Well, I think that's enough time spent here Mr Walling don't you? Shall I show you the Count House?

WALLING: Very well ... but ... a ... Mr Tamblyn ... was giving me some new insights...

WILLIAM: I think Mr Tamblyn should probably be getting back to his duties...

JIMMY: Right on sir, Cap'n Tresawna. Nice talking to you Mr Walling ... Shall we be seeing you again, like?

WALLING: I don't think so. Back in Plymouth, the editor has got me lined up for some post in the war.

JIMMY: What, reporting on the battles? Now, I tellee wha'. You wudn' see me goin' in there with paper an' pen. I'd at least wunt a dabber an' a pickaxe ... A bit ov that there explosive charge from down Number Eight wud be quite helpful too...

WALLING: Something like that. The way things are goin', a western front 'll be opening soon. You've got to take these chances. They don't come round very often ... It won't last long. I'm sure of that. Look Mr ... ah rather ... Cap'n Tresawna. I think I have all I need. I really must be travelling back to Plymouth. You've been very accommodating. The article should be in this week sometime. You should like what I have to say. Cheerio to you both. Oh – but before I go, a photograph I think ... The benevolent Cap'n with one of his workers ... Would you mind?

JIMMY *and* WILLIAM *come together awkwardly;* JIMMY *smiling and* WILLIAM *frowning.* WILLIAM *eventually squeezes out a smile.*

WALLING: Could you ... just squeeze in ... yes ... a bit more Mr Tresawna .. Wonderful. Shake hands I think...

WALLING *takes the photograph with a puff of flash.*

WALLING: Excellent that does the trick. Nice to have met you...

WALLING *exits.*

JIMMY: Not a bad bloke all told ... Brave an' posh ... but then ... thaas buggers from up the line fur 'ee. Always knaw better than you do...

WILLIAM: I hope you didn' speak out of line back there James Tamblyn.

JIMMY: Me? Cap'n Tresawna ... I never spoke out of line all my life.

JIMMY *smiles and turns, showing his crossed fingers to the audience.*

WILLIAM: Good. Now show me where you an' John Henery have set the charges. I want to double-check them, an' see how the lad's getting' on.

WILLIAM *and* JIMMY *enter the shaft. 'Hail to the Homeland' is first heard, and then fades.*

4. The exterior of the North Wheal Leisure Mine, 2 July 1914.

It is later the same week. JOHN HENRY PASCOE *enters, holding a piece of paper.*

JOHN HENRY: [*reads*] "Wanted, Cornishmen!" Good that ennet? "What we want for the Duke of Cornwall's Light Infantry are Cornishman. At present, a very small percentage of the Regiment are Cornishman. Still, of that small percentage many posts have been held by Cornishmen [*looks at audience*] during the last few years in the Cornish regiment. A Cornishman [*shakes head in disbelief*] who enlists in the Regiment is made doubly welcome, and from the fact that he is a Cornishman, has every enducement to be promoted. It is the hope and ambition of all the Officers of the Regiment that the Regiment should be for Cornishmen [*scratches head*], as it was many years ago in the days of the siege of Lucknow, where the Cornish miner proved his worth. If parents who wanted a really good career for their sons, would communicate privately with the Officer Commanding the Depot at Bodmin, he would be delighted to give them all the information about life in the Cornish Regiment. God save the King!" Me? Na. I'm too young ... You got to be sixteen. But Jimmy...

JIMMY *enters carrying a rock drill over his left shoulder. The rock drill could almost be a machine gun.*

JOHN HENRY: Well, the way things are goin' back North Wheal Leisure, I d'reckon Jimmy'll talk himself out ov a job if 'ee dun't blaw hisself up first. I'll give ut to un.

JIMMY: That right is ut? An' give what to me?

JOHN HENRY: Er ... this ...

JIMMY: What is it?

JOHN HENRY: Dunno. Recruiting poster...

JIMMY: Duke of Cornwall's is it?

JOHN HENRY: Yeah...

JIMMY: Well, they 'ent a bad bunch all told, but you wun't catch me joinin' up there ... not less I was really desperate ... I'd rather head out t'Grass Valley if I was honest; price ov gold what 'tis. Good money to be made out there...

JOHN HENRY: An' what if it's not a choice...

JIMMY: What 'ee mean? Conscription...

JOHN HENRY: Yeah?

JIMMY: It wun't come t'tha' ... Tell 'ee wha' though ... I 'eard tell the Reverend Joseph Hocking's comin' to Perranporth. Recruitment drive for the British Expeditionary Force...

JOHN HENRY: Goin' t'see un?

JIMMY: 'Spect so. Well, 'ee be famous, inna'? 'Spect 'ee'll be like all the rest ov um though. Fight the good fight an' tha' – but they'm home here. They wun't be dabbered up in some 'ole fightin' they Germans. Same as Kitchener and all the rest ov um...

JOHN HENRY: So you 'ent goin' t'join' up?

JIMMY: No. I'd be as likely t'join up as Polmassick'll make a straight bit ov timberin'. All these glory-seekers. You'll find me right at the back of the queue, stankin' over moor in the opposite direction. 'Ere, talkin' of which ... woz all this I hear bout you an' some maid up Garnbargus?

JOHN HENRY: Nothun'.

JIMMY: Nothun'?

JOHN HENRY: Yeah. Nothun'.

JIMMY: You'm a dark horse, you, John Henry Pascoe...

JOHN HENRY *smiles.*

JIMMY: Good fur you. A boy your age needs a maid. Mother knaw yet do she?

JOHN HENRY: Naw ... not yet.

JIMMY: Dun't 'ee worry? I wun't tell nobody ... You knaw I'n always keep a secret.

JOHN HENRY: Really?

JIMMY: 'Course ... [*running and shouting*] Never guess what! Boy Pascoe only gone an' got hisself a maid ... Tell the world ... Come on you ... We'm goin' pub t'celebrate ... Get 'em in Johnny. 'Tis 'Coming-off-Shift-Special' o'clock ... Bewdie...

5. The 'Western Daily Mercury' newspaper office, Plymouth, 2 July, 1914.

Night-time. The dull light of a newspaper office. A spotlight on the table. An ashtray next to it. ROBERT WALLING *is sat at a table, on top of which is a heavy, large iron typewriter.* WALLING *is tall, thin and genial. He is bashing down the keys on the machine to construct his story, every so often looking at his notes in his notebook. He draws on a cigarette as he types.*

WALLING: [*speed-reading his own writing*] The town of Perranporth seems a long way away from the dramatic events shaping Western Europe, but in fact, what goes on in this small Cornish parish, can alter Britain's war effort.

MRS SLATTERY *enters backwards through the door, carrying several documents, talking to her boss, and the 'Western Daily Mercury' editor, Mr Higgins.* MRS SLATTERY *is in her late 50s.*

MRS SLATTERY: [*deferentially*] I will do, Mr Higgins. Of course ... Absolutely no problem at all.

MRS SLATTERY *shuts the door.*

MRS SLATTERY: [*in correct English*] Oh ...You're working late Mr Walling?

WALLING: Trying to finish this stupid mining story Mrs Slattery ... you know, the one I went to see earlier this week...

MRS SLATTERY: You'd have thought there were enough other events going on at the moment without us looking at some paltry Cornish tin mine.

WALLING: Mr Higgins doesn't seem to think it's stupid. Besides, local angle's important, he says. Doesn't want to be seen dropping the local news in favour of all the foreign drama ... and he's keeping the hatches, matches and dispatches.

MRS SLATTERY: Read me some.

WALLING: [*reads*] Cap-tain Will-i-am Tresaw-na is a man whom the Cornish say has a nose for tin. He commented, 'This mine is the finest in Cornwall. In a few weeks, when the new headframe is up, we shall be the most efficient as well.'

MRS SLATTERY: I've heard the Captains down there rule with a rod of iron.

WALLING: They do ... I mean, they do own the place ... That's the way it is.

MRS SLATTERY: Sounds wrong to me. Well, the Cornish have clotted cream for brains.

WALLING: Listen ... as you're here, Mrs Slattery, would you very much mind taking a letter for me? To go tomorrow morning? It's only brief...

MRS SLATTERY: Young man, such items are for the typing pool ... but very well. Seniors don't normally do this kind of thing.

MRS SLATTERY *sits and takes a pad of paper, ready for* WALLING'*s dictation.*

MRS SLATTERY: To whom is it going?

WALLING *stands up, taking a small green-bound book from his desk. As he dictates, he flicks through the book.*

WALLING: Mr Henry Jenner.

MRS SLATTERY: Address?

WALLING: The British Museum, London.

WALLING *pauses, looking in detail at the pages of the book he carries.*

MRS SLATTERY: A-hem ... I'm waiting, Mr Walling...

WALLING: Oh sorry ... yes ... Dear Mr Jenner ... I hope this letter finds you well. I was delighted to receive in the post this week, your book, 'A Handbook of the Cornish Language'...

MRS SLATTERY: Cornish, did you say?

WALLING: Why yes ... the Cornish language...

MRS SLATTERY: They always think they're better than the rest of us, those Cornish ... That's the last thing we need at the moment. These barbarians telling us they're different somehow. That's why it all started over there in Austria. I suppose everyone'll have to speak this confounded Cornish one day.

WALLING: [*frustrated*] Look ... Mrs Slattery ... I know you have your views, but just take down this will you? [*dictating again*] I found the book a fascinating read, and am hopeful (the present war willing) to complete a series of articles upon it. I have Cornish ancestry on my mother's side, and so could relate to much of what you said. Perhaps ... Perhaps when you are next in Hayle I might come and interview you. Given your rules of grammar and initial dictionary, I am so inclined to learn alongside to you, so I might one day converse with you.

MRS SLATTERY: [*incredulous*] Are you serious, Mr Walling?

WALLING: Of course.

MRS SLATTERY: What, learning a dead language? And may I remind you young man, this is a newspaper office, not a language school.

WALLING: It's no longer dead. At least, not according to Mr Jenner.

MRS SLATTERY: Who is this Mr Jenner anyway? To me, you're learning a dead language in a time of death ... If the damned Cornish wanted it kept going, they should have kept on using it years ago. Now, is that it? Yours faithfully, ... etc etc ...?

WALLING: No, not quite ... Hold on ... I wrote this earlier: *Kimmyas kres dewheles dhe'n bys arta whare.*

MRS SLATTERY *looks at the audience in amazement.*

MRS SLATTERY: That Russian is it? Or is it from Outer Mongolia. Can you spell it for me?

WALLING: K–I–double M–Y–A–S...

MRS SLATTERY: Give it here. What does it mean?

MRS SLATTERY *snatches it, and copies it into her notes.*

WALLING: May peace return to the world again – soon.

MRS SLATTERY: Very poetic I'm sure. Mr Asquith would be proud of that. You can say modern things then in this 'Cornish' ... To my mind, it would much better if the whole world spoke English. Stop all the wars that would. Do you require the translation to be included?

WALLING: No need. He'll know ... Sometimes sentiment is much better in another tongue.

MRS SLATTERY: Very well. I will do it first thing in the morning and place it in the post for you, Mr Walling.

WALLING: Thank you Mrs Slattery.

WALLING *moves to switch off the desk light.*

MRS SLATTERY: Now, as for that other matter you were discussing with Mr Higgins ... Special Correspondent with the Duke of Cornwall's ... He told me to tell you. It seems you may be going sooner than we thought ... They're going out with part of the Expeditionary Force ... Pioneer group. Are you still the man for the job?

WALLING: Yes ... yes ... I believe so, Mrs Slattery...

MRS SLATTERY: Very well. Mr Higgins wants you leaving next week. Looks like you won't be having much time to learn any of that language of Mr Jenner's then? Fortunately. Oh ... and make sure that tin mine article is finished will you? I know you've grander things on your mind, but final copy is final copy, Mr Walling...

WALLING *switches the desk light off.* WALLING *and* MRS SLATTERY *start to leave.* WALLING *turns back. He switches the desk light on again, and picks up the green book. He leaves. Music: 'Hail to the Homeland', with snatches of Euphoric trance. It ends when* ROSE PASCOE *slams down her mixing bowl.*

6. The kitchen of the Pascoe household, Pencrennow Farm, 7 July, 1914.

ROSE PASCOE *is at work, in the kitchen. She has a traditional white-centred cream mixing bowl on the table, with a yeast-bun mix inside it. She stirs the mixture frantically, with a wooden spoon, adding sultanas. Cornish blue and white crockery are on the table. Two places are laid out for tea. Ten already cooked yeast buns are laid out on a griddle. There is a knock at the door.* ROSE *wipes her hands and straightens her hair. She opens the door. It is* WILLIAM.

ROSE: Cap'n Tresawna? A nice surprise...

WILLIAM: Well, I was passing by Pencrennow ... so...

ROSE: So...

WILLIAM: So ... thought I'd pop in t'see you, Mrs Pascoe ... Always a pleasure. Never a chore...

ROSE: Well ... always good to see you...

WILLIAM: Something smells good...

ROSE: Baking ... yeast buns ... One lot out of the oven, look see. Another being made up ... And beef stew (with dumplings) on fur tea ... fur John Henry... 'Ave one. Go on. Plenty ov nubbies fur 'ee.

ROSE *offers him the griddle.* WILLIAM *takes one and starts to eat it.*

ROSE: Nice piece in the paper Cap'n Tresawna ... 'bout the mine an' that...

WILLIAM: Not bad ... Not bad ... Of course, not that keen on some of the reporting that chap did ... Journalists do have a way of exaggerating the negative ... Blowin' things out of all proportion you might say. Still thaas what they'm paid fur ... I s'pose. The mundane doesn't sell papers.

ROSE: Like this war thing ... Trouble's brewing, I'n tell.

WILLIAM: Well ... perhaps so ... perhaps so ... Hard to know what'll happen ... All we can be is prepared I s'pause...

ROSE: So you dun't think it'll come this far? – or affect the mine? You said so in the paper.

WILLIAM: To tell the truth, Mrs Pascoe ... I don't know. I hope not.

Pause, while this sinks in. WILLIAM *eats the yeast bun.*

WILLIAM: John Henry not back yet?

ROSE: Not yet. Chasing some maid down village, I spect. I d'reckon 'ee've someone in mind. I told un to be back fur his tea by six. I must ask: how's a getting' on then? A couple of months now ennet – since 'ee started.

WILLIAM: Good, so I hear, from James Tamblyn. Tamblyn 'ent 'zactly the model tributer fur un, but 'ee do knaw the ropes. 'Ee had him chargin' the lines this week ... A serious job that ... He'll make a fine Cap'n I d'reckon ... one of these days...

Beat.

ROSE: Really. My John Henry chargin' lines. I'd never have believed ut. Will 'ee stay fur your tea Cap'n Tresawna? It's just tha'...

WILLIAM: No ... no really ... I should be gettin' back home.

ROSE: You can ... 'Twun't take me a minute just t'put a bit more stew on ... The dumplings'll only take a while to cook...

WILLIAM: No ... I have work to do. I must prepare a report for the shareholders. Then, by the weekend, I must be in Bodmin...

ROSE: Bodmin ... Whatever for? Long way to go traipsin' up there...

WILLIAM: Business, Mrs Pascoe. Business, of some importance. National importance you might even say.

ROSE: I see ... aw ... some business...

WILLIAM: Er ... yes ... I shall be back for chapel Sunday morning. Will I see you there, Mrs Pascoe? It's always ... always ... just tha'...

ROSE: I 'spect so. 'Tis anniversary soon ... and there's a lot to do. Books to buy fur attendence, and the readings to be rehearsed. Must get some of they there Hocking novels in.

WILLIAM: 'Course...

ROSE: No rest for the wicked, as they d'say.

WILLIAM: Well, I'll be off then ... Lovely yeast bun by the way ... As good as they always are...

ROSE: Right ... Well...

WILLIAM: I'm right aren't I? [*beat*] This weekend. [*beat*] Archie's death wudn' ut? On the 50 fathom ... timbering wudn' ut?

ROSE: [*broken*] 'Es ... the 50 fathom level. Timberin'. Ten year ago now...

WILLIAM: Not just chapel anniversary then...

ROSE: No – other anniversaries too. Funny how there are more and more as you get older, eh, Cap'n Tresawna? Sometimes I think thaas all dates are fur on the calendar ... to fill in when people 'ave passed away on. Poor souls.

WILLIAM: If ever you want to talk ... I'm...

ROSE: [*recovering*] I appreciate the offer Cap'n Tresawna. I do. But there idn' much you'n say. Not much anyone can say really ... I wudn' the fust housewife in Cornwall t'lose a man to the mine, and I shan't be the last – thaas fur shure. Time be a good healer I d'reckon.

WILLIAM: 'Es – well, the best healer is always time ... I'll be off then...

WILLIAM *is just about though the door, when he is stopped by* ROSE'*s words.*

ROSE: What the newspaper said ... 'tis right idn' ut? Things be safer now ... below ground ... I mean 'twas bad enough when I was at bal and spalling ... so ... stands to reason I'm worried...

WILLIAM: 'Tis safer now, fur certain, Mrs Pascoe.

ROSE: John Henry see ... 'Ee's all I got now ... I cen't 'ave 'ee taken too...

WILLIAM: I know...

ROSE: Goodnight then Cap'n Tresawna...

WILLIAM: Night ... [*pause*] Rose...

ROSE *comes to the table again. She crumples, crying into the yeast bun mixture. A transition: Her sobs quieten and merge into the sound of waves crashing upon a shore. This matches a projection of barrelling waves breaking. Hear the swash of water through pebbles and stones.*

7. The sand dunes, Perranporth, 10 July, 1914.

The waves merge into the sound of a seagull. We hear the sound of excited voices off-stage, involved in a game of chase.

GIRL: [*teasingly*] Stop it ... John Henry ... No ... You're tickling me...

JOHN HENRY: I thought you liked it though...

GIRL: [*flirtatiously*] What if I do?

JOHN HENRY: [*laughing*] Then I'll do it some more...

A hot summer's day. The GIRL *runs breathlessly on stage, adjusting her dress, looking guilty. The* GIRL *is carrying a blanket and picnic basket.*

GIRL: [*shouting off-stage*] Here, this'll do...

The GIRL *spreads the blanket on the floor, and holds the basket with both hands.* JOHN HENRY *runs on, firing a hard-head at her.*

JOHN HENRY: [*out of breath*] God ... you can run some fast ... I keep missing you...

GIRL: 'Course I can ... Come on. Sit down. I've made we a picnic ... I've got saffron cakes, and see, look, Fairings biscuits ... and a flask of sugary tea...

Beat.

GIRL: It won't hurt you John Henry – to be sittin' in the dunes on a Sunday afternoon, with a girl, politely eatin' of some sandwiches ... What would your mother say of you, sat up here with me?

JOHN HENRY: She wudn' mind...

GIRL: Really ... what, on a Sunday too, when you should be at home a-reading Matthew, Mark, Luke and John from the Good Book.

JOHN HENRY: She's too busy with changin' the flewers back the chapel to notice we.

GIRL: Too busy with Cap'n Tresawna I d'reckon ... You knaw 'ee got a soft spot for her.

22

JOHN HENRY: [*defensive*] No 'ee 'ent.

GIRL: 'Course 'ee has. Everybody d'knaw that ... The whole ov the parish d'knaw that. I've seen ut. It's the way 'ee looks at her ... [*laughing*] All that deep, unreleased passion kept under control beneath 'is bowler hat.

JOHN HENRY: Do 'ee think so?

GIRL: [*laughing*] 'Course.

JOHN HENRY: After ... I mean ... when ... I dun't think she would look at another man ... It's not her way ... not now.

GIRL: 'Course she would. She dun't want t'end up lonely. Nobody wants t'end up lonely. Here, eat this...

The GIRL *opens the basket and hands out sandwiches wrapped in grease-proof paper.*

GIRL: I got some cheese an' a bit of piccalilli.

JOHN HENRY: Tamblyn says Tresawna's cracked ... Too many years in the dark 'ee d'reckon ... either that or 'is brain poisoned by arsenic...

GIRL: Jimmy Tamblyn! And what d'ee knaw? He 'ent nothun' special ... 'Ee d'think 'ee's God's gift. Father said he knawed tin backalong, but not any more ... Dun't you be listening too much to 'ee, when you'm workin' up mine. Jimmy Tamblyn think 'ee got the world hold of by the asshole. Truth is, 'ee dun't knaw very much...

JOHN HENRY: 'Ee's been good to me. Showed me the ropes. Learnt me how to stope. How to set charges an' tha'.

GIRL: Dare say 'ee has ... but dun't treat is word as gospel. 'Ee dun't even go Chapel no more ... Come t'think ov ut, 'ee've never been Chapel – not so as I've see'd.

JOHN HENRY: I know. 'Ee says it idn' fur un. 'Ee an' John Wesley wudn' meant to meet – someun' like tha'. Said 'ee was too much ov a wrestler an' a smuggler to be following the path to righteousness. Cup tea?

GIRL: Please. An' what about you John Henry – what do you want outta' life?

Beat. The GIRL *and* JOHN *Henry turn and lie down upon their backs.*

JOHN HENRY: Nothun' much. Just t'be happy ...'Ent that what moast people d'want?

GIRL: Thaas as good as any wish, though men these days usually want more than that. That there assassin in Serajevo he wanted more didn' he? Some ideal ... some aim ... and all 'ee brought about was somebody a-dying...

JOHN HENRY: Not me. I just want to work up the mine. Maybe one day think about being a Cap'n – if I d'learn well 'nough...

GIRL: [*dreamily*] Cap'n John Henry Pascoe – sounds good ... sounds proper. Like it belonged t'be.

JOHN HENRY: And you? What do you want?

GIRL: Everything. I want everything ... I should want everything. I mean, it's a new century – why not? They say women will have it all this century ... not like it used to be...

JOHN HENRY: You can't have everything ... I d'knaw that.

GIRL: No. But you can have moast things...

JOHN HENRY: Moast things maybe...

Beat.

JOHN HENRY: So as I've learnt so far in life, sometimes it's best not to be too ambitious. That way, y'wun't be disappointed ... An' if some'un do 'appen, well, perhaps 'tis all planned out fur 'ee.

Beat.

GIRL: [*sarcastic*] Jimmy Tamblyn teach 'ee that?

JOHN HENRY: No. That's me. John Henry Pascoe, famous Perranporth philosopher.

Beat. The GIRL *smiles and sits up.*

GIRL: Look at the ocean. Shimmering. Looks as if it's not got a care in the world.

JOHN *sits up and looks.*

GIRL: I wish I could be out there on it.

JOHN HENRY: Wha' – in a boat?

GIRL: No – riding the white horses ... going with the flow of the waves ... feeling them press against me. The energy of ut.

JOHN HENRY: I like the water. I have to go there, have to, after a shift like. When we've come to grass, I like to smell the salt. I went there when faather wuz killed ... 'tis like a medicine fur the soul I d'reckon. When Jimmy goes down the pub, I always head out to the coast, to walk there. Then you can pretend you wun't be spendin' your next core stoping over head again.

GIRL: I've been going there to forget.

JOHN HENRY: Forget what?

GIRL: This 'ere war that's building, Johnny.

JOHN HENRY: Do you have to go on about it? How do you know anyway?

GIRL: No. I don't have to.

JOHN HENRY: Then don't. Just watch the sea with me.

Beat.

GIRL: Did I tell 'ee? My brother's thinking of volunteering.

JOHN HENRY: Really?

GIRL: Yeah – up Bodmin – the Duke of Cornwall's Light Infantry ... There's a call gone out for Pioneers. There's posters up in the village. Notices in the paper. Joseph Hocking's speaking down village too.

JOHN HENRY: The paper's say it'll be over soon though. We had this journalist come to the mine. He said so. That's wha' 'ee told, Jimmy.

GIRL: Maybe ... I don't know though ... Sometimes I think the world has wars just to let itself know pain again ... Like when you bite your finger-nail, and it bleeds ... [*turning anxiously to him*] Promise me you won't sign up John Henry...

JOHN HENRY: I won't. I promise.

GIRL: Because...

JOHN HENRY: Because what?

GIRL: You know why.

The GIRL begins to pack away the picnic items.

JOHN HENRY: Is this why?

The Girl and JOHN *look intensely at each other. John and the Girl kiss. The Girl breaks from him.*

GIRL: John Henry! Never knew you had it in you...

JOHN HENRY: I've learnt more than mining off Tamblyn ... Come on, I'll race you to the Cross...

GIRL: No you won't. I'll beat you to the Cross every time.

JOHN HENRY: Wanna' bet? You know what, you'm properly mazed sometimes...

GIRL: So are you boy Pasca' ... Come on ... give me a decent snog y'bugger.

The GIRL *and* JOHN HENRY *kiss again; this time falling to the ground. The lights fade.*

8. Tywarnhayle Square, Perranporth, 15 July, 1914.

A podium. Aim to get the audience to stand, so they are part of REVEREND JOSEPH HOCKING's *crowd.* HOCKING *does not wear a dog-collar, but is smartly dressed for the occasion.* JIMMY, JOHN HENRY *and the* GIRL *push through the audience.*

JIMMY: Make 'iss will 'ee? I dun' wun't t'be late ... fur Mr Hocking's speech...

JOHN HENRY: Who' is a anyway?

GIRL: You dun't knaw who Joseph Hocking is? Well, 'ee be that writer-bloke.

JIMMY: Some speaker they d'say ... Voice like an angel. Honest. Bit ov a Methodee do-gooder ... Rumour is, 'ee've bought Bodvean House up Droskyn...

JOHN HENRY: Still dun't knaw un.

JIMMY: 'Course you do. Think back t'anniversaries when you was a boy ... 'Spect you got presented with one of 'is novels ... All the fashion back then, you. Father got whacks of 'is books. Said 'ee used t'read 'em of a night in some bunkhouse in Africee. Reminded un ov 'ome 'ee used t'say. Aw ... look out ... Tresawna's on...

JIMMY, JOHN HENRY *and the* GIRL *push to the front.*

26

WILLIAM: Now, Ladies and Gentleman, boys and girls of Perranzabuloe, I've no need to tell you who our guest is. I am sure you all know Reverend Joseph Hocking, preacher and novelist. I am certain many of you have read his books, full of adventure as they are...

JIMMY: Get on with ut y'wind-bag...

WILLIAM: ...They are without doubt books to put you on the straight and narrow, but he is here tonight, to speak on a rather more urgent request concerning the present conflict. I give you Reverend Joseph Hocking.

The crowd claps. WILLIAM *gets the audience to join in.*

HOCKING: Thank you Cap'n Tresawna. It is, indeed, a great pleasure to stand before you tonight. I should like to talk more about my books, which I know many of you have read, but I come to your parish today under rather more serious circumstances. It is true that Europe is at war. It is true that our country is in jeopardy. But it is also true that time and time again, the Cornish have served their country well. The Cornish are a very clannish people and are suspicious of strangers. But I am a Cornishman. I know you all. I am acquainted with your history, your characteristics, your language. And I know that recruiting is going well here. However, tonight I come before you to raise your Celtic fire. There is still a need for more brave young men to take up arms against the enemy.

WILLIAM *claps loudly.* JIMMY *looks around to see who the brave, young men are.*

JIMMY: You tell um Mr 'Ocking!!! You tell um...

HOCKING: Many of our finest men are already in France. And yet if only we had more men, we could put Germany and its allies to rout. That is our great need. More men like the Duke of Cornwall's Light Infantry, who have already covered themselves with glory. You should hear what the men at the front are saying about those who are hanging back. They are a disgrace to the country. If ever God called you to fight in a Holy War, it is now. And this is the heart of my message to you all tonight. Whatever profession you are in: be it mining, fishing or farming, think of this day which you will be able to look back on, and say proudly that you fought for freedom and justice. I say to all the young men here, there are NCOs and officers in the Tywarnhayle

Inn who will enlist you tonight, so tomorrow you may be travelling to the front to do bit. Let us fight this greater evil, and pray to God, let us win.

WILLIAM *leads the shaking of* HOCKING's *hand, and escorts him down.*

WILLIAM: A fine speech Reverend Hocking ... I'm sure we'll see an increase...

HOCKING: Well, thank you Cap'n Tresawna. One hopes for the best, for the good of the country.

WILLIAM: Of course...

JIMMY *pushes through to* REVEREND JOSEPH HOCKING.

JIMMY: Now you spoke un' good an' true there Mr 'Ocking ... I agree with all you d'say bout fightun a greater evil ... Tell 'ee what though ... how 'bout your fur me son here? This is a first edition ov your novel Jabez Easterbrook. I've read ut cover to cover ten times...

JOHN HENRY *tries to protest.* JIMMY *covers* JOHN HENRY's *mouth and produces a copy of the novel.*

JOHN HENRY: [*muffled*] I 'ent his son.

REVEREND JOSEPH HOCKING *signs.*

JIMMY: [*starstuck*] Thank 'ee kindly Mr 'Ocking. I shall treasure tha' and so will the boy 'ere ... 'Tidn very often we d'ave the likes of you round here...

WILLIAM *puts out his arm to shield* REVEREND JOSEPH HOCKING *from* JIMMY, *and escorts him off.*

WILLIAM: Shall we?

JIMMY *looks at the signature in his book.*

JIMMY: [*reading with great satisfaction*] Fight the good fight. Best wishes, Joseph Hocking.

JOHN HENRY: So – you signing up?

JIMMY: 'Course not. I 'ent no lamb to the slaughter ... I'm off fur a pint ... Comin'?

JIMMY *leaves. The* GIRL *comes over.*

GIRL: Will 'ee walk me 'ome, John Henry?

JOHN HENRY *becomes very shy.* JIMMY *returns.*

JIMMY: Go on! Walk 'er 'ome ... I would...

JOHN HENRY: 'Course...

The GIRL *takes* JOHN HENRY'S *hand. Very slowly, she moves to kiss him.*

GIRL: Come on ... the moon's up ... Let's walk by the surf. I knaw you like ut there.

JOHN HENRY *and the* GIRL *leave.*

9. Shaft No. 6 at North Wheal Leisure Mine, Perranporth, 12 August, 1914.

The sound of a compressed air hard-rock drill at full tilt inside the shaft. JOHN HENRY *is passing several stick fuses into the shaft, for use inside. He checks a sticking tommy is lit.* JIMMY *is inside singing 'The White Rose', badly.* WILLIAM TRESAWNA *enters, watching the activity.*

JOHN HENRY: A'right Cap'n?

WILLIAM: What 'ee on upon?

JOHN HENRY: We'm a ... just ... stopin' back ... Mr Tamblyn 'ave a ... got a plan ... see.

WILLIAM: Have a now?

JOHN HENRY: Aw yes ... Always got a plan...

JIMMY: [*shouting from within*] Who's tha' out there? Tidn' that figgity hummity Tresawna be ut? It 'tis, tell un where t'go will 'ee?

WILLIAM *listens, smugly smiling to himself.*

JOHN HENRY: [*worried, shouting in*] You'd best come out, I think, Jimmy...

JIMMY *comes out. He is supping from a bottle of Brown Ale. He puts the lid on and hides it in his pocket, wiping his his mouth with his sleeve. In his other hand are a couple of fuses.*

JIMMY: What you lookin' at?

WILLIAM: I'm lookin' at they fuses you'm holdin' in yer hand. New ones idn' um from Nobels?

JIMMY: Nobels. 'Es. An' what ov ut?

WILLIAM: They'm plenty strong. Thaas all. An' I'm worried...

JIMMY: Worried ... Fur who? Not 'bout me. You've never worried bout me much Cap'n. Any danger down mine, an' you'm always, "Get in Boy Tamblyn. 'Ee'll do ut ... 'Ee's mad, bad and dangerous enough." So when've you been worried 'bout me?

WILLIAM: You – yes, course I'm worried 'bout you ... but tidn' just you now es ut? You've your pard t'think 'bout.

JIMMY: Aw ... the boy ... I see ... Perhaps tidn' 'ee t'all. Perhaps 'tis more his mawther. 'Ee's 'appy with ut. Trust un wun't 'ee? I shawed un.

Beat.

WILLIAM: And I'm telling you Tamblyn, that be too much. Mark my words...

JIMMY: [*with passion*] Gaa. Tresawna. You knaw, as well as I do, I've been drilling stopes here at North Wheal Leisure more times than you've had hot dinners. You dun't tell me how t'do ut! I d'knaw how t'do ut, and you d'knaw that.

WILLIAM: [*controlled*] Dun't I? I warned you about this last blastun' on the 30 fathom level. Would 'ee take notice of me? I tell 'ee, I prayed fur 'ee down there – what with you and the boy just along the shaft. Any ov ut could 'ave come in on top ov 'ee. But would 'ee listen. Naw – you wudn listen because you'm Jimmy bleddy Tamblyn ... World expert...

JIMMY: I dun't need naw praying fur. I dun't need none ov your hypocrit-ical Methodee-ism canorical nonsense neither. I knaw all about you Bill Tresawna ... You think you'm the big I am round here, hob-nob-bin' ut up with Joseph Hocking, but you 'ent ... None of the boys like 'ee ... In fact, they 'ent got a good word t'say about 'ee ... [*whispering*] And yeah, all that time you d'spend up Mrs Pascoe's, lookin t'get under 'er skirt. Bet she dun't knaw 'bout that time her Archie was working on your core do she? Aw naw. Dun't 'spect she do. An' now, nobody ben't goin't'say a word are um – what with her boy on the core?

WILLIAM: You'll never change Tamblyn ... Always been the same ... Just like yer faathur. Wasted all the money 'ee made on the Rand. Come home broke didna? Not a penny on un. Had t'start over again, as a timberman. Like faathur, like son. Thaas wha' I d'say. Tell me how much you've pissed up 'gainst the wall down the Tywarnhayle ... or wasted on cards, an' coursin', an' women...

JIMMY: I tell 'ee straight Bill Tresawna. You may be Cap'n ov moast of the men but you'll never be my Cap'n – not ever ... I d'hear you moaning on about the resurrection, and redemption every Sunday ... but tha' dun' come to men like me ... I'm beyond all tha' see. I knaw me place ... an' tidn' up there with angels and cherubs and harps. Aw naw. 'Tis down there below, deep in the earth, 'mongst the mineral canopies an' burnin' hot fathoms where Beelzebub and the devils are toastin' my poor soul on the sumpshaft, an' prodin' me on the racking. 'Tis an awful wisht job t'say ut, but I've never, in my whole born days, worked fur such a clicky-handed cussel ov crud as 'ee, Cap'n.

WILLIAM: Well you, you cudn' catch cold off a quilkin, even if you tried.

JIMMY: And you'm stiffer than Barker's Knee...

WILLIAM: If I'm tha', well, I'n see, you an' me's goin' t'have a goodly ding dong.

In each other's faces.

JIMMY: See Cap'n, I d'reckon you'm blacker than the devil's crowst bag!

WILLIAM: Well, you might be strong in the arm, but you'm weak in the 'ead, you g'eat clob stanker!

JIMMY: Gaa – I may be a clob stanker, but you, you be blunt as a dag, and as mazed as curlew. Like St Agnes Whitetide fair: full ov gidgees and gliddering. Ghastly tempered an' the more I knaw 'ee ... the more I've gone back on 'ee...

WILLIAM: You ... You ... You ... drilgeying dunkey wrangler...

Beat.

JIMMY: [*utterly incensed*] Drilgeying dunkey wrangler! Well ... Thaas the best you'n do es ut? Well, well, Bill, you must be losin' yer touch. I'm serious. If you wanna' stop me, Cap'n, you goin' t'ave t'scat me ass over tip ... Now, if you'll excuse me, I'm goin' in, and I may be some time.

WILLIAM: Let the boy out then...

JIMMY: 'Ee's comin' out Cap'n. 'Ee's got the plunger.

WILLIAM: [*to himself*] We must all die, even an' when God pleases...

JIMMY: Sa far as I knaw ... I've set un good an' proper, an ol' boy ere is full obm'.

WILLIAM: [*shouting in, concerned*] You cover yerself now John Henery. Yer mawther ud never forgive me else...

Controlled, WILLIAM *swaps his bowler hat for a miner's hard hat, and mouthing the numbers silently, counts down from 10 to 0. Meanwhile,* JOHN HENRY *comes out with an electrical exploder (detonator). He turns a handle on it to make a siren, and then winds it up to make the charge.*

JIMMY: [*from inside*] We'm on, you ... 'Es ... [*gleefully*] We'm on ... I'n see the tin glistening ... When you'm ready John Henry ... Push un down ... Pretend 'tis the soft bosom of that maid you'm seeing. Hold un gently between your hands, an' ease un down...

JOHN HENRY *slowly pushes down the detonation plunger. There is an enormous explosion. A blackout. Rocks and dust are catapulted outside of the shaft. The last thing to come rolling out of the shaft is* JIMMY's *broken helmet.*

JOHN HENRY: [*frantic*] Jimmy! Jimmy! You hear me?

JOHN HENRY *enters the shaft to save* JIMMY.

WILLIAM: [*collected and controlled, dusting himself down*] Let the bugger stay there ... Thaas what I say. The idiot put enough explosive in there t'blaw up half ov Perranzabuloe parish. Maybe a bit of mundic rock hittin' 'is head will knock some sense into un. Would a listen? Na 'ee wudn'...

John Henry: Cap'n! Cap'n! I'n 'ear ov un groanin'. 'Ee be in there thankin' the Lord 'ee idn' deaded.

WILLIAM: 'Ee be an atheist! Whatever's wrong widn'?

JOHN HENRY: The timber's 'ave gone ... The whole level's gone in on un...

WILLIAM: Can us get to un?

JOHN HENRY: 'Es – if we'n eave a 'undredweight ov rock out the way.

WILLIAM: You go back up t' the dryin' room. Fetch any men you can. Get um down here, quick she like. Give us that shovel.

JOHN HENRY *passes him a Cornish shovel.* WILLIAM *shows a side to him that we have not seen before: that of an experienced man in the face of adversity. He takes off his jacket, rolls up his sleeves and strides into the tunnel.*

WILLIAM: I'n hear 'ee, y'drilgeying donkey. Hold fire! Pray t'the Lord you've been saved, and I'll have 'ee out Jimmy ... Dun't 'ee worry.

JIMMY: [*weakly*] I love you Cap'n.

WILLIAM: Dunnee start any ov that nonsense you hear! Dun't worry. You'll be down the Wink a'fore you know ut ... No man goes down when I'm Day Cap'n.

We hear the scrape of the shovel on rock, and of the superhuman strength of WILLIAM. *Grunts and groans come from the shaft as material is moved to release* JIMMY.

WILLIAM: Can 'ee see light as yet?

JIMMY: Not yet. Keep diggin'. Eh, Cap'n, they fuses got a bit ov poke to um edn' they?

WILLIAM: Like I said...

JIMMY: An' thaas why you'm Cap'n and I b'aint. Tell 'ee wha' though ... there's a fine bit ov tin been brought down. Keep we goin' fur a bit...

WILLIAM: Never mind tha'. Give us your hand.

More dust and rock fall as JIMMY *and* WILLIAM *emerge,* WILLIAM *staggering with the weight of* JIMMY.

JIMMY: Well ... I wudn' have believe tha' if I'd seen ut in the West Briton. A God-fearin' man such as you, savin' a sinner such as me.

WILLIAM: Hurt be 'ee?

JIMMY *checks himself just to make sure.*

JIMMY: Nothing hurted. Only me pride.

WILLIAM: Well, they d'say pride do come before a fall. Come on ... Leave ut fur now. Let's go get cleaned up.

JIMMY *places his hand on* WILLIAM's *shoulder.*

JIMMY: Cap'n, 'onest t'God, I do awe 'ee one...

WILLIAM harshly brushes JIMMY's hand away.

WILLIAM: Maybe Jimmy, but I gotta' tell 'ee boy, thaas the last time you'll work North Wheal Leisure.

JIMMY: What 'ee mean?

WILLIAM: You'm too much of a liability Tamblyn. You never follow the rules. Rules is everything in my book.

At this, more dust emerges out of the shaft. WILLIAM turns away and dusts off his bowler hat, and puts on his dress-coat. WILLIAM exits stage left. JIMMY feels in his pocket. Miraculously, the bottle of Brown Ale has survived. He unscrews the lid and takes a satisfying sip.

JIMMY: Aaah...

JOHN HENRY hurriedly enters from stage right, coming to a surprised standstill.

JOHN HENRY: You made ut? You got out...

JIMMY: 'Es. You cen't keep a good man down.

JOHN HENRY: Tresawna?

JIMMY: Fur once in his life, 'ee used a shovel...

JOHN HENRY examines the chaos of the shaft.

JOHN HENRY: Shallus carry on? There's a goodly bit ov tin in there. Brave an' easy t' get to now.

JIMMY: You'll be there by yerself John Henry.

JOHN HENRY: Wha' 'ee mean?

JIMMY: [*sniffs regretfully*] Been given me marchin' orders...

JOHN HENRY: But you an' me? We'm pards 'ent us?

JIMMY: 'Es. Pards still. [*beat*] Only not here.

JOHN HENRY: Whaas' yer plan?

JIMMY: 'Ebm got no plan. See 'ee later, John Henry.

JIMMY leaves stage right. JOHN HENRY is left alone. He moves to a still-lit sticking tommy and blows it out. In the blackout, a transition into next scene.

10. The Duke of Cornwall Light Infantry Depot, Bodmin, 15 September, 1914.

Military music plays. We hear the sound of marching on gravel. There are piles of sandbags (later used in the trenches) and munitions on the floor. Some rifles, pick-axes and shovels. The COMMANDING OFFICER *enters, marching briskly. He carries a cane, and a briefcase, and on entering, he tests a surface on the set for dust. Everything is completed by the book. Everything is positioned on the table at right angles. He looks at his wristwatch. Precisely, as he does this, there is a knock on the door.*

OFFICER: Enter.

The figure at the door does not come in. The figure knocks again.

OFFICER: [*loudly*] Enter!

The door opens and a flustered JIMMY TAMBLYN *enters. He is carrying a suitcase.*

JIMMY: This the right plaace is ut?

OFFICER: For what?

JIMMY: Joinin' up?

OFFICER: If you are considering offering your allegiance to the heroic cause of the present war, and fight against the dreaded Boche, then yes, [*beat*] you are in right place.

JIMMY: Jimmy Tamblyn ... Come up on the train ... from Trura ... I seen the Reverend Joseph Hocking speak in Perranporth ... A passionate man an' naw mistake. 'Ee said you needed men ... an' given tha' my present position 'ave expired of late ... I thought ... I might try me luck in the DCLI...

OFFICER: I see. [*conspiratorially*] You a [*whispering*] Cornishman?

JIMMY: Yeah – I am a [*whispering*] Cornishman...

OFFICER: [*whispering*] Have to be damned careful. Not many of us about these days.

JIMMY: [*knowingly, pointing to his nose*] I wun't say a word...

OFFICER: Well, as the poster says, [*loudly and prouldy*] a Cornishman who enlists in the Regiment will be made doubly welcome, and from the fact that he is a Cornishman, has every enducement to be promoted.

JIMMY: Promotion? Sounds good to me, boy ... er... sir...

OFFICER: Please, take a seat. I just have to take a few details. Shouldn't take a moment. Name?

JIMMY: James Tamblyn.

OFFICER: Age?

JIMMY: [*trying to sound more soldierly*] Twenty-six, sah.

OFFICER: Address?

JIMMY: [*coughs*] I'd rather not say, sir...

OFFICER: Rather not say? Shall I put 'of no fixed abode'?

JIMMY: Women ... See ... I dun't 'zactly knaw where I be residin' at this present moment in time ... ahem ... at the present ... Can 'ee just put down Perranporth?

OFFICER: Perranporth?

JIMMY: With two Ps...

OFFICER: Employment?

JIMMY: Tin miner ... Tributer ... sort of ... 'till last week...

OFFICER: Really? You may come in very handy. Always on the look out for miners at the front ... for the pioneers, you know.

JIMMY: Yeah?

OFFICER: Tunnelling, lad. Excavations under the enemy's positions. Dashed hard thing to do, but the Duke of Cornwall's got a bit of an advantage there. Mining stock, see. There at Harfleur ... Agincourt ... Lucknow ... and now again in 1914. 'Once more into the breach' and all that, eh?

JIMMY: I 'ent bad with a bit ov explosive. If I'n blaw a ninety tonner under Wheal Leisure, then I d'reckon I'n plan an excavation and drop a tasty mine or two in there...

OFFICER: Well, I think that's about it really Mr Tamblyn. If only there were more men like you in Cornwall. One and all, what?

JIMMY: So I'm in?

OFFICER: Of course. Sign here.

JIMMY *signs.*

OFFICER: Congratulations.

The OFFICER *shakes* JIMMY's *hand.*

JIMMY: What now?

OFFICER: Follow the corridor. Quartermaster's Stores. They'll soon have you kitted out. Bit of a medical. Shouldn't be a problem. Tongue out. Quick cough. Check your John Thomas: standard procedure, and then you're set. Basic training. British Expeditionary Force. Your draft leaves in a fortnight.

JIMMY leaves. The OFFICER *signs the recruitment form and stamps it. He positions everything on the table at right angles again. He looks at his wristwatch. Precisely, as he does this, there is a knock on the door.*

OFFICER: Enter.

The door opens. A figure enters wearing a cap. The figure's form is familiar, though he is wearing a coat intended to make him look older. It is JOHN HENRY PASCOE. *He carries a suitcase.*

OFFICER: How can I help?

JOHN HENRY: I've come to enlist.

OFFICER: Jolly good. [*conspiratorially*] You a [*whispering*] Cornishman?

JOHN HENRY: [*puzzled*] Yeah – I am a [*whispering*] Cornishman...

OFFICER: [*whispering*] Have to be damned careful. Not many of us about these days. Some are impersonators too. Need to be careful with the Kaiser about. [*beat*] Name?

JOHN HENRY: John Henry Pascoe.

OFFICER: Address?

JOHN HENRY: [*in hard-core Cornu-English*] Pencrennow Farm, Perranzabuloe, Cornwall.

OFFICER: Somewhat Cornish then ... [*beat*] Age?

JOHN HENRY: [*Beat*] Seventeen.

OFFICER: Seventeen? Sure about that?

JOHN HENRY: Yes.

OFFICER: Do your parents know you've enlisted?

JOHN HENRY: Mother, sir ... I've only me mother...

OFFICER: Mother then ... Does she approve?

JOHN HENRY: I told her so. Not sure she d'approve, but tidn' her decision, sir.

OFFICER: I see.

JOHN HENRY: She'll come round to the idea. I d'reckon sodgerin's just as dangerous as minin' anyways.

OFFICER: You've mining experience?

JOHN HENRY: Sir, these past few months, I been apprenticed at mine.

OFFICER: You know how to wield a pick and gad then?

JOHN HENRY: Yes sir. The Cap'n there will give you good reference of my work, sir.

OFFICER: I don't think there's any need for that ... Besides you'll need to wield a bayonet and rifle just as well now. Just sign here please...

JOHN HENRY *signs the recruitment form.*

OFFICER: Follow the corridor. Quartermaster's Stores. They'll soon have you kitted out. Bit of a medical. Shouldn't be a problem. Tongue out. Quick cough. Check your John Thomas: standard procedure, and then you're set. Basic training. British Expeditionary Force. Your draft leaves in a fortnight.

JOHN HENRY: Thanks.

JOHN HENRY *makes his way, dissolute, across the stage. The* OFFICER *straightens his desk, then stands and exits through the door. As* JOHN HENRY *is crossing,* JIMMY *returns, carrying a huge and unstable pile of military clothing. The two cross and turn.*

JIMMY: Na...

JOHN HENRY: Yeah...

JIMMY: Na ... Tha' 'ent you John Henry, be ut?

JOHN HENRY: [*taking off his cap*] It is.

JIMMY: In the depot? Dun't tell me...

JOHN HENRY: I've enlisted.

JIMMY: Enlisted? You? You 'ent hardly old enough t'go Trura ov a night – let alone travel up here t'a place s'full ov vagabonds an' thieves as Bodmin...

JOHN HENRY: I could say the same ov you. You'm meant t'be me pard Jimmy. You didn't even tell no one where you'd gone...

JIMMY: Well ... thought I'd best be dun with mining after that little bit ov smoak I made! Didn' have much choice did I? Sodgering's best of a bad lot I d'reckon. But listen ... wha' about your maid? D'she knaw you've joined up?

JOHN HENRY: She dun't knaw nothun'. I'll write t'she.

JIMMY: You'll break her heart...

JOHN HENRY: She needn't knaw ... not yet...

JIMMY: An' mawther? She knaw I s'pause...

JOHN HENRY *doesn't answer.*

JIMMY: Not mawther neether?

JOHN HENRY *looks down sheepishly.*

JIMMY: You'll break 'er 'eart and 'er mind too. So, Tresawna, 'ee d'knaw dun't a? I mean, you must've told 'ee...

JOHN HENRY *shakes his head.*

JIMMY: Wha'!? You didn't tell 'ee ... You just walked out mine? Well, dun' 'ee think you'll get your job back when all this mazed fisticuffs is soon over.

JOHN HENRY: I knaw.

JIMMY: So what in 'ell are 'ee thinkin' ov? Joining up ... 'tidn a game you knaw...

JOHN HENRY: Didn' want to break our pard-nership Jimmy – not after I'd learnt s'much.

JIMMY: [*seriously*] You write t'mawther mind. An' tha' maid. From what I've see ov she, she's worth keepin' ... Bugger Tresawna though ... 'Ee's one boy I wun't be missing...

JOHN HENRY: I went down beach ... yesterday morning ... just to see the waves come in ... in case...

JOHN HENRY and JIMMY gaze into mid-distance, as if looking out on the Atlantic Ocean from Perran Beach. A brief revival of the projection of the sea.

JIMMY: In case... 'es ... in case...

JOHN HENRY: Could be a while...

As they contemplate their fate, the door opens. A man dressed in military uniform enters. There is a familiarity about him. As they talk he stands behind them.

JIMMY: 'Es ... six months, they d'reckon ... Over by Christmas though.

JOHN HENRY: Wonder if we be in the Pioneer ranks together...

JIMMY: The old crew back, eh?

JOHN HENRY: You'n stack as much fuse in as y'like Jimmy ... Blaw the Boche buggers up that will...

JIMMY: Reckon I will John Henry ... Reckon I will...

The figure behind them speaks.

WILLIAM: Reckon you will boys.

JIMMY: Who's tha'?

WILLIAM: Your Section Cap'n.

JIMMY: Section ... Cap'n ... [*under his breath*] I didn' come here fur no bleddy Cap'n. Had enough of the last Cap'n orderin' me around...

WILLIAM: What was that, Private?

JIMMY: Nothun, Cap'n.

WILLIAM: 'Ten'shun!

JIMMY and JOHN HENRY stand to attention, their eyes almost shut. JIMMY accidentally drops his new military uniform.

WILLIAM: So, do I not recognise you pair from another life?

JOHN HENRY: Dun't think so Cap'n, sir ... We'n from down west.

WILLIAM: I think I might ... Safety fuses ... Brown ale ... Dunkeys ... Ring any bells t'all ?

JIMMY: Hang on a minute. I d'recognise that voice anywhere...

Very slowly, JIMMY *turns his head around and looks at* WILLIAM TRESAWNA, *this time dressed as a Captain in the Duke of Cornwall's Light Infantry.*

JIMMY: Na ... John Henry ... It can't be ... They need un down North Wheal Leisure. Why the hell would a be up here in Bodmin? Better people to recruit than 'ee, yeah? 'Tis me worst nightmare. Let me home. I want me dunkey.

JIMMY *looks again. The threat is real. He turns to the audience, his eyes wide open with fear and loathing.*

JIMMY: Tell me it 'ent true. Tell me it 'ent true. [*to audience*] Is ut true? Is ut true? That Tresawna?

WILLIAM: While you, Tamblyn, have been wastin' your hours on wine, women and song, I, William Garfield Tresawna have been training with the Duke of Cornwall's Light Infantry at the Bodmin Depot for several years now. And now you bring your low, vile life to me once again, for me to make a soldier of you ... The irony of ut, eh, Jimmy Tamblyn?

JIMMY: 'Es. 'Tis a bit weird, now you come to mention it. Don't s'pause you'n keep us in the back like ... where it 'ent too dangerous...

WILLIAM: Nothun' we'n do about ut now. You've signed up and you'm in my section ... but you, John Henery, I'm surprised at you...

JIMMY: [*before John Henry can even speak*] Boy idn' even old enough ... He be only fifteen, Cap'n ... Send the poor lad 'ome. 'Ee'n start shovelling out tha' stope we started. That maid ov 'is can look after un. His mawther'll be pleased. If you go 'ome too, well ... Mrs Pascoe'll be in cherks!

WILLIAM: 'Ee idn' goin' anywhere. Who am I to question the lad? If 'ee wants to sign up, let un. It'll make a man ov un! 'Ee idn' the only one. I 'ent goin' anywhere either.

JIMMY: Well, look like we'm goin' t'be one happy family ... Shame we'm goin' off t'war...

WILLIAM: Time you was off to your billets for the night. You'm on the

Duke of Cornwall's core now m'lads! Left right, left right, left right...

JIMMY *picks up the fatigues he dropped earlier.*

JIMMY: [*to John Henry*] I just 'ope 'ee be betterin' at sodgering than 'ee be at mining. Then we might have a drop ov hope.

JIMMY *and* JOHN HENRY *exit.* WILLIAM *pauses, considers the fate he must now endure, then exits. Fade in 'Hail to the Homeland'.*

Act Two

1. A Communications Trench, near the Somme, 3 July, 1915.

Dawn. A handcuffed JOHN HENRY *is marched on stage by* WILLIAM TRESAWNA, *who is carrying a blanket and blindfolding materials. He is led to an execution post (a shell-destroyed tree), and tied there.* WALLING *enters as an observer, taking notes as the execution proceeds. As* JOHN HENRY *speaks,* WILLIAM *blindfolds him.*

JOHN HENRY: [*desperately*] Oh mother... mother...

The Flanders skies are full of stars,
and the earth is cold as clay.
I'll be shot dead at dawn
and buried six foot deep, by end of day.

WILLIAM: Call in the men.

The sound of a seagull, who has come in from the sea. As the VOICEOVER *is read, an unwilling* JIMMY *enters as the firing squad.*

VOICE: [*off*] Private No. 2120, John Henry Pascoe, Duke of Cornwall's Light Infantry, has been charged and found guilty of when on active service, of shamefully abandoning post in the presence of the enemy. He has been convicted and sentenced to death. This sentence has been confirmed by Field Marshal Sir John French, Commander-in-Chief, British Expeditionary Force, and will be carried out at dawn on 3rd July 1915.

WILLIAM *nods at the firing squad. He raises a white hankerchief. This is the cue for the firing squad to charge their rifles.*

JIMMY: [*unable to help himself, weeping*] Sure you wun't do this Tresawna?

JOHN HENRY: [*to himself, quietly*]

43

And shall Trelawny live?
And shall Trelawny die?
Here's twenty thousand Cornish men
Will know the reason why!

WILLIAM *lowers his handkerchief.*

The sound of rifle fire, and its echo. For a second, JOHN HENRY's *body barely moves, then the head drops. For a brief moment: a split stage –* ROSE PASCOE *at the table making yeast buns. She stops her cooking as the shot rings out, knowing something is wrong in some distant place.*

WILLIAM: Use the blanket.

JIMMY *crosses the stage and transfers* JOHN HENRY's *body onto the blanket.* WILLIAM *exits.*

WILLIAM: [*still strong*] Bury the body will you? In the next field.

JIMMY: Pards to the end, eh? I'll dig fur 'ee boy – one last time.

JIMMY *exits dragging* JOHN HENRY's *body behind him.* WALLING *exits.*

2. Abandoned North Wheal Leisure Mine, Perranporth, Cornwall, at the start of the twenty-first century.

Euphoria music. MAISIE *enters by clambering on top of the mine shaft. She is wearing a pink surfing hoodie and surf-print skirt, with Ugg boots. Her entry is matched by a projection of the ocean. She walks to the end of the shaft and sits down. In her bag is a lap-top computer. She takes it out and switches it on as she talks. She also takes out a Ginsters Pasty and a can of Red Bull. As* MAISIE *talks, figures clad in great-coats, balaclavas, and tin helmets assemble the trench set to her left.*

MAISIE: So, you know that boy? Well, I met up with him ... Yeah, I cudn' believe it either. Turns out he's a'right. So we went for a few drinks, an' we're kind ov seeing each other. Nothing heavy. He 'ent like the normal kind of idiots down there. Yeah – an' 'ee's studying at Plymouth Uni. Environmental Science, specialising in Marine Ecology. "Very trendy," I says to him. That's why he's started surfing – according to him – "to get to know the ocean". "Might want to get some lessons first," I said. "Can you teach me then?" he says to me. So I said I would, when he's next down. So now we're MSNing and tex-ting – you know like a couple ov daft kids. He's sweet – might be a keeper. He even burned me a CD with all these songs on it that reminded him of me. You never know ... But that ain't the plan, right? I mean the plan is get me degree, then go off travelling. Yeah. I wanna' surf a bit of the world. You know all the legendary places: Haiwaii, Australia, Costa Rica, California ... oh yeah, and Porthtowan ... Surf the seven seas. Got to earn some money first though. Save up a bit. God, I feel some knackered ... I was out late last night ... there was a party over Aggie.

MAISIE *opens the can of Red Bull and drinks from it.*

MAISIE: That's why I'm up here. To clear me head. And sometimes I come here to write. No distractions see. We've got an essay to do. Research project for end of the First Year. You've got to investigate some aspect of history that had a local impact. Do some fieldwork. Go to library. Do not pass go. Do not collect two hundred pounds. Well, I'm not sure what to do. An' like always, I've stupidly left it t'the last minute. I'm a real numpty that way. Gotta' get more organised – but you know what it's like. Too many other distractions.

MAISIE *opens the Ginsters Pasty and begins to eat it.*

MAISIE: I mean, I was thinking of looking at the collapse of the world tin price and the effect on North Wheal Leisure. Yeah – I know! Sounds way interesting that does, doesn't it? I mean how many other twenty-year-olds have an interest in the growth and decline of the Cornish tin mining industry. I must have a t-shirt with 'Complete Nerd' written on it. Then again, my mum was on about the First World War. Said there was some interesting stories from the parish: about the Tommies who fought. Her gran was on about it. I'll go and have a look down the War Memorial later on. It's bad enough with what's goin' on in Iraq and Afghanistan an' tha' – but that one. Well, when y'hear about it, it's like the numbers of dead were unbelievable. It always amazes me at human beings' incredible capacity t'bring disaster upon themselves. And what's history? The more I read, the more I think that it's about mistakes repeating themselves. Giant cycles of time re-occurring. Like we never learn...

The light gradually fades down on MAISIE, *who starts to check her e-mails, and comes up on* JOHN HENRY *and* JIMMY *marching in, now clad in full military fatigues. If possible, this should include khaki jacket and trousers, webbing, great coats, balaclavas, steel helmets. They also carry Lee Enfield rifles, shovels and cigarettes.* MAISIE *exits.*

3. Excavation tunnel and trench at Mons, 12 November, 1914.

We hear the distant crunch of heavy artillery. The full extent of the trench is now seen. The shaft has been transformed into an excavation tunnel. Now, there are piles of military equipment, a munitions box on which the pioneers sit. A look-out ladder rests against the side of the trench. Through the scene a uniformed and highly-armoured ROBERT WALLING *is a constant presence, taking notes on all that he sees. Both* JIMMY *and* JOHN HENRY *are already mud-splattered, and singing to keep up their spirits.*

JIMMY and JOHN HENRY [*singing*]:

A good sword and a trusty hand!
A merry heart and true!
King James's men shall understand
What Cornish lads can do.

And have they fixed the where and when?
And shall Trelawny die?
Here's twenty thousand Cornish men
Will know the reason why!

CAPTAIN WILLIAM TRESAWNA *enters. He is dressed like* JIMMY *and* JOHN HENRY. JIMMY *and* JOHN HENRY *take off their great-coats and helmets.*

WILLIAM: The where and when's right here. One more effort and we should be right under the Hun's lines. Private Tamblyn, Private Pasca', you'm on tunnelling crew again...

JIMMY: Again?

WILLIAM: No choice. The Runner from Command told me what we've been asked to work on. [*noticing Walling*] Oh – morning, Mr Walling?

WALLING: Cap'n Tresawna ... Seems we are fated to be together? Alright if I just...?

JIMMY: Still scribblin' notes, I see.

WILLIAM: Carry you ahead.

JIMMY: [*overlapping*] Cap'n, I'm telling ov 'ee. If we go any deeper in there we shall be comin' up in Australia ... It d'play 'ell with your nudduck.

JOHN HENRY: Sir, the tunnels is gettin' some small under the German lines. Even I'n barely get in there now. We must have moved near on hundred kibbles out yesterday...

JIMMY: All I'm sayin' is tha' just fur once, 'twould be nice t'be out in the fresh air, Cap'n Tresawna ... We'm 'ere fur a lubbet an' thaas all.

WILLIAM: But you boys are used to this. Would you rather you were goin' over the top then? Facing the wrath of some Hun Maxim gun or *minenwerfer* – t'lie dying on barbed wire?

JIMMY: Well, when you put ut like tha' ... I'll take the galleries any day. Cen't odds ut.

JOHN HENRY: 'Tis the clay here Cap'n. The ground idn' like 'tis back home. There, 'tis solid – you knaw where you are. 'Ere, well, 'tis slippery and you'm skiddering all over the shop. You need more support because ov ut.

JIMMY: 'Tidn' easy doin' ov ut quietly either. I swear yes'day I heard a German party goin' in over the top ov we...

JOHN HENRY: We need more bellows Cap'n – t'pump more air in. 'Tis gettin' hard t'breathe down there. The Monoxide's playin' 'ell on us.

WILLIAM: I'll make sure more bellows are brought up. Private Tamblyn, can you see if you can hear where the enemy is. We might consider blawin' it later today.

JIMMY: You blaw there Cap'n and they'll hear it go up back Perranporth. 'Twill be like an earthquake across the whole ov Europe...

WILLIAM: Well, boys, we may not make 'istory, but we shall certainly change the geography.

JIMMY: There'll be nothun' left ov Mons, Cap'n. You'd better look to see where our boys is too. We dun't want t'put mines under they. Best make a start then...

JIMMY enters the excavation tunnel, picking up a few bars of 'Trelawny', as he grabs a pick axe. WILLIAM converses with JOHN HENRY.

WILLIAM: 'Eard from mother 'ave 'ee?

JOHN HENRY: A letter, last week...

WILLIAM: She a'right?

JOHN HENRY: Goin' chapel a lot, so she say. She be a'prayin' for you an' me every night...

47

WILLIAM: I must write to her.

JOHN HENRY: She'd like that, I d'reckon.

WILLIAM: I miss her.

JOHN HENRY: [*direct*] She be missin' you too. I d'think, Cap'n, that when we'm back 'ome ... you might want t'ask her to marry 'ee.

WILLIAM *is befuddled and suddenly self-conscious of his love.*

WILLIAM: I'm not sure she'd...

JOHN HENRY: You been round our house years now ... She d'make 'ee yeast buns regular-like. Someun's on. Nothun' would please she more.

WILLIAM: You're right. I'll write to her. Yes ... tonight...

JIMMY *sticks his head out of the tunnel.*

JIMMY: Cap'n, you better come an' 'ave a geek... I dun't want no repeat of that little incident we 'ad back home...

WILLIAM: Comin'...

JOHN HENRY *starts to enter the excavations, but stops as* WILLIAM *asks him a question.*

WILLIAM: John Henery – your maid...?

JOHN HENRY: Mother've got to knaw er. Sharin' the same experience ben't um?

WILLIAM: Does she write?

JOHN HENRY: Yeah...

WILLIAM: Do you write back?

JOHN HENRY: Naw. I d'reckon she'll knaw I'm a'right s'long as they dun't get no telegram. Besides, so I've learnt, there's things out here 'tis best not t'write 'bout ... Knaw what I mean, Cap'n Tresawna...

WILLIAM *knowingly nods.*

JIMMY: [*from inside*] You pair comin' or no?

JOHN HENRY: Right behind 'ee boy...

JIMMY, JOHN HENRY and WILLIAM *enter the tunnel, and leave the stage at the rear.* ROBERT WALLING *is left alone on stage, talking to himself as he writes a letter. He sits down on the munitions box, continuing to scribble. We do not hear the whole of the letter, but selections during the composition process.*

WALLING: November 18th, Dear Henry, I hope this note finds you and Kitty well. I am following the Duke of Cornwall's, so I am, at least observing the Cornish in action... [*continues writing, and then under his breath*] I am told one of the Captain here is a man I interviewed at Perranporth. [*continues writing*] My editor wants more human interest stories from the front. He tells me I must be in the action .... Please send me any more articles on the language. I am hopeful that I am becoming more fluent. In a while, I hope to send you something of great interest that I write here in the excavations. *Co-mer-o whee-th.* Robert Walling. Ah yes, a PS. PS Is the Cornish word for war, *bressel*? I believe here we have *an bressel mear*!

WALLING *writes an address on the envelope, places the note inside and licks it to seal it.*

WALLING: [*noticing the tunnel*] Ah ... the excavations. I'm sure Tresawna's laid out his new captaincy here.

With considerable trepidation, WALLING *enters the excavation.*

4. The kitchen of the Pascoe household, Pencrennow Farm, 12 November, 1914.

A snippet of 'Hail to the Homeland'. The kitchen is dimly lit. MRS PASCOE *is on the toilet, so we see just her feet. The* GIRL *is at the table. The mood is of quiet desperation.*

GIRL: [*calling over*] Mrs Pasca'... See this in the Western Daily Mercury... There's a report by that journalist who came by North Wheal Leisure. Mr Walling, thaas 'is name. 'Ee's with the Duke of Cornwall's, giving dispatches home. There's progress at Mons, he reckons. The pioneers is tunnelling under the German positions. If they do ut, they'll progress to Wipers. I knaw you dun't want t'knaw about ut all, but I 'ave to. I need t'knaw what John Henry's goin' though out there. If I knaw wozon, then I can manage ut. [*to Mrs Pascoe*] I'm sure Cap'n Tresawna's a'right. You know, 'ee's a good man. A good leader. 'Ee won't put 'em inta any harm – not if 'ee can

49

'elp ut. Mrs Pasca, you 'earin' ov me? [*pause*] There's more being called up y'knaw. Bet that Reverend Hocking've been busy. 'Twill come t'conscription soon. Thaas wha' my brother d'reckon. [*beat*] Look, do 'ee 'ear ov this: one of these stupid advertisements. "Young Women of Cornwall". Thaas me I s'pause. "Is your best boy wearing Khaki?" Well, yeah, me best boy is wearin' khaki so see, 'ee idn' ere. "If not, don't you think he should be?" Personally, no. I dun't think 'ee shud 'ave even volunteered, but thaas John Henry fur 'ee. Proper bull-'eaded, see. Cen't tell un nothun' – then again, you'd knaw that wunnee' Mrs P? "If he does not think that you and your country are worth fighting for – do you think he is worthy of you?" "Don't pity the girl who is alone – her young man is probably a soldier – fighting for her and her country, and for YOU." [*laughs*] Hear tha' Mrs Pasca'? They'm not t'pity we. [*pause, then a sigh*] I wish ee'd write. Has Cap'n written you? If only I 'ad word; somethun' t'gaw un. [*beat*] Listen, I'd better go. I'm off down beach. Dun't 'ee worry Mrs Pasca'... They'll be a'right...

The GIRL *leaves. The lights darken.*

5. A trench system, Flanders, near Ypres, 5 January, 1915.

It is snowing. JIMMY *and* JOHN HENRY *are cold, trying to keep warm.* WILLIAM TRESAWNA *enters with the very formal-looking* CORPORAL CHRISTIAAN VAN DER RIET. JIMMY *and* JOHN HENRY *stand to attention, and salute* CAPTAIN TRESAWNA *and the* CORPORAL. WILLIAM *and* CHRISTIAAN *salute back.*

WILLIAM: Morning men. Now that the Duke of Cornwall's made it back and forth through Mons, the Spring campaign takes us north to Ypres. Our work on the excavations was highly commended. Now, Command is seeking for us to make a break-through there by March. More 60-pounders and 4.5 inch howitzers. Therefore our company will be supporting the front line. Training with the Vickers machine gun. In short, less excavation work; more combat. Haig's putting everyone forward for a real surge on the enemy. The offensive will be hard, but should put an end to matters.

JIMMY: [*to John Henry*] Jesus ... 'Ere ov un ... Surges an' offensives to Wipers, as if 'ee knaw what 'ee's talking about...

WILLIAM: Your initial role in the front-line trenches will be supporting those already there: lining trenches and so on, and nightly missions to cut barbed wire.

JIMMY: [*a sarcastic aside*] Jus' like goin' through the vuzz up moors.

WILLIAM: Now to assist our company, I would like to introduce you Corporal Christiaan van der Riet. Our advancement is dependent on our allies in the Colonies.

CHRISTIAAN *steps forward.*

CHRISTIAAN: [*in strong South African accent*] Good morning men. You from Cornwall, yes...? My old toppie worked with the Cornish in the gold-mines back home. [*Enthusiastically*] I reckon I've scored a moerse goal working with you.

WILLIAM: Corporal van der Riet is from the 1st Battalion, South African Volunteer Rifles, and has been assigned to work with us on the offensive. The First have considerable experience in dealing with barbed wire, at the Battle of Loos. I shouldn't have to tell you it was the First who pioneered the successful use of chlorine on the enemy there.

JIMMY: Gas?

CHRISTIAAN: Aaah where. Chlorine gas...

JIMMY: I thought we weren't using any ov tha'...

WILLIAM: Have to ... The enemy is ... We have to fight fire with fire...

JOHN HENRY: So, Corporal, what'll 'ee be doin' with us then?

CHRISTIAAN: Bru, training you louse-ridden droë wors up so you can cut the moffie's wire under darkness...

WILLIAM: By the way Corporal, Command has detailed Mr Walling to be accompanying you as your correspondent. They want good morale-boosting stories sent back to the papers ... You know the kind of thing. Right, I'll leave you to get started.

As WILLIAM *leaves, the demeanour of* CHRISTIAAN *completely alters.*

CHRISTIAAN: I wasn't expectin' no scrompie like that.

JIMMY: Listen... 'Ee's alright ... An' Mr Walling will tell ut true ... 'Ee's a good ol' boy too. Always scribblin' away like naw tomorra'...

CHRISTIAAN: Right, now that the Captain's out of the way ... let's take it easy. It's swak I got to train you boys. Anyone got any cigarettes or beer?

JIMMY: I got beer. I always got beer.

JOHN HENRY: I've got some ciggies from my rations.

CHRISTIAAN: Jislaaik! Let's have a bit of a party, eh boys? Fetch the braai. That Tresawna eh? I could klap him in the face...

JIMMY *instantly takes a liking to what suddenly seems like a co-conspirator against* WILLIAM TRESAWNA. JOHN HENRY *also relishes the prospect of rest and relaxation.*

JIMMY: My faather worked in South Africa ... At De Beers, first of all. Then at Kimberley...

CHRISTIAAN: Kimberley? That's where my toppie worked with the Cornish. Moses Roberts used to organise a One and All Cornish Diner, yeah? My toppie always went. City and Surburban, eh? Then there was the Ferreira out on the Veldt. Lots of Cousin Jacks there...

JOHN HENRY: You knew some Jacks then?

CHRISTIAAN: 'Course I did ... Listen, when this bosheraad's over, I'm leggin' it back to the Transvaal. Lekker gold there boys. You wanna' come over...

CHRISTIAAN *and* JIMMY *and start to smoke and drink. Their spirits are high.* JOHN HENRY *is not quite so comfortable with this world, and we see him separate off from the other two.*

JIMMY: A good life there then?

CHRISTIAAN: Ag, man. You'll never be bergie there. Tell you what, the place is filled with broekie too.

JIMMY: Wha'? You 'ent speakin' Cornish there are 'ee?

CHRISTIAAN: Broekie? – Women...

JIMMY: [*suddenly realising*] Ah, muzzie ... Caw d'ell. I 'ebm had a bit of muzzie or broekie fur months ... Hear that John Henry, the maids are some good-lookin' over South Africee...

JOHN HENRY: Uh...

CHRISTIAAN: Yeah. [*making an hour-glass female shape with is hands*]

Especially down on the beach ... in the summer ... You know how it is... [*dirty gesture*]

JIMMY *and* CHRISTIAAN *stop, realising their banter may have gone a step too far for* JOHN HENRY.

JIMMY: You d'knaw John Henry ... You like to go down beach dunnee'?

JOHN HENRY: We got beaches back 'ome, yeah. I d'like goin' out there.

CHRISTIAAN: Yeah – but does your broekie go there, right? Well back home, they go down to watch us surfing.

JOHN HENRY *and* JIMMY *look at each other in puzzlement.*

JOHN HENRY and JIMMY: Surfing?

CHRISTIAAN: Eina! You know, on boards. On the ocean. It's kwai, yeah?

JOHN HENRY: What 'ee mean?

CHRISTIAAN: It hits you in the soul. It's simple right. You get a plank of wood, and you swim out on it into the waves. So then you trek for a bit right, and wait for the best wave. And when that waves comes past, you stand on the board. Nooit – it's unbelievable ... Yeah – so when I'm here in Flanders and away from home, that's what I think of.

JOHN HENRY: [*incredulous*] Standin' on a board. In the middle of the sea. Wha', like walkin' on water, eh? Sounds wonderful.

CHRISTIAAN: Yeah. You got to be skort, else you'll fall off. Ag, man ... Let me teach you Tommies.

It is still snowing, but CHRISTIAAN *searches around for pieces of duck board.*

CHRISTIAAN: Get on the board, like this, yeah?

JIMMY *and* JOHN HENRY *imitate* CHRISTIAAN.

CHRISTIAAN: Bakgat! That's it...

JIMMY: Ooh – we'm havin' some rigs 'ere! They'd rise tail afore if they cud see we back Bolingey!

The three start to pretend surf in the trench. Euphoria music. The projection shows the ocean waves. WILLIAM TRESAWNA *enters stiffly.*

WILLIAM: What you party doin' ov? Look like you'm dancing' sum purty on pieces ov duckboard.

Cut Euphoria music. JOHN HENRY, JIMMY *and* CHRISTIAAN *freeze, arms and legs askew.* JIMMY *hides the beer he is holding.*

JIMMY: [*slightly drunken*] Eina! Nooit! Broekie ... A'right Cap'n Tresawna ... The Corporal be just showin' us ... a technique, yeah, ov getting' across ... bits ov barbed wire...

CHRISTIAAN: We did this at the Battle of Loos. Nice little manoeuvre, yeah?

CHRISTIAAN *combines his surf moves with some wire cutting.* WILLIAM *shakes his head and leaves.*

WILLIAM: [*to himself*] Crazy colonials...

JIMMY: Watch him...

CHRISTIAAN: That poep don't bother me. You gotta' try it man ... in Cornwall ... I guess the waves there are very good ... Right in off the Atlantic, eh?

JOHN HENRY: I'm goin' do ut when I get back ... Me an' you Jimmy – on the Atlantic?

JIMMY: Yoh ... I'm doin' ov ut. Look at me...

CHRISTIAAN *claps and drinks from his beer.*

CHRISTIAAN: Good fun, eh? Come on, let's get into the dug-out. Rum and biscuits? We'll keep Tresawna happy, an' put a plan in place yeah?

CHRISTIAAN *leaves.* JOHN HENRY *and* JIMMY *are left alone.* JIMMY *puts his arm around* JOHN HENRY'S *shoulder.*

JIMMY: Dunnee take no notice of all they manly rigs we had there. Tell 'ee what boy, you an' me – out on the waves when we get back, eh? I promise.

JOHN HENRY: Bewdie Jimmy. That'll be some proper.

JOHN HENRY *starts to walk into the dug-out.*

JIMMY: 'Ere boy, I'm always 'ere fur 'ee. Remember that pard.

They leave to enter the dug-out. Their voices continue and then fade.

JOHN HENRY: Corp, where do ut come from then?

CHRISTIAN: Surfing? Depends on who you talk to ... Some people say Polynesia ... But definitely Hawaii.

JIMMY: How do 'ee make the boards?

CHRISTIAAN: They made them out of redwood on Waikiki Beach, yeah? Then balsa for a while ...Yeah ... then back home, we got these paddle-boards and aqua-gliders.

Fade in the Methodist minister VOICEOVER.

VOICEOVER: They that go down to the sea in ships that do business in great waters: These see the works of the Lord, and his wonders in the deep. For he commandeth, and raiseth the stormy wind, which lifteth up the waves thereof. They mount up to the heavens, they go down to the depths: their soul is melted because of trouble.

Lights fade to black.

6. The streets of St Omer, 14 February, 1915.

JOHN HENRY *on his own in the trench. He is carefully making something out of a piece of metal. When he holds it up, we see it is a copper heart. Simultaneously, a red light.* MICHELLE MÉHAUTÉ *enters. She is a Belgian Lady of the Night, finding rich pickings in the rest time of the British Army in Flanders. A drunken* JIMMY TAMBLYN *enters.*

JIMMY: [*to audience*] Stayin' back 'ere in billet fur a few days. I been yaf-flun' down a few pints of piss. Said to ol' boy t'come inta town with me, but 'ee wudn' 'ave any ov ut. [*pause*] I worry 'bout un. 'Ee've been awful quieted ov late. [*beat*] Still, it ov been a while since tha' maid back Bolingey. I need me a bit ov muzzie ... or broekie... This 'ere maid d'look purty... Maybe I can use a bit ov the ol' Tamblyn charm...

MICHELLE: [*impatient*] L'Anglais is as pissed as a Pole...

JIMMY *comes up and politely shakes* MICHELLE'*s hand.*

JIMMY: Put it there maid. Jimmy Tamblyn. Master miner ... an' tunneller ov Flanders ... In town from the front, for one night only.

MICHELLE: Are you English? You want to make the love?

JIMMY: [*to audience*] Direct here idn um? 'Tidn even like this back the alley next t' Market Inn in Trura ... [*to Michelle*] My 'andsome ... I got-ta' tell 'ee, I idn' English...

MICHELLE: You part of ze English army, yes?

JIMMY: Might be part ov ut ... But I 'ent English ... Never 'ave been. Never will be. I be ov the Duke of Cornwall's ... A Cornishman ... Accordin' to that there Mr Walling, I should be proud ov tha'...

MICHELLE: I do not mind ...Cornish, English, no matter. We still jiggy-jig, yes? Have you money?

JIMMY: Plenty ov money, 'es... Would 'ee like to accompany me to a bar fur some convivial refreshment? I like ze *romance, oui*?

MICHELLE: To a bar? Not to a room?

JIMMY: Well, what've you got in mind my bewdie?

MICHELLE *approaches* JIMMY *and slides her stockinged leg over* JIMMY, *whispering in his ear.*

Michelle: You are romantic? You know ... a long time for you in the trenches ... Maybe we sleep together? War makes men and women lonely ... *Oui*?

JIMMY: You serious maid?

MICHELLE: *Oui*. If you are...

JIMMY: [*to audience*] 'Spect if you take the paint off her, she edn' no more than a fryin' pan fulla' assholes ... but beggars cen't be choosers in wartime ... besides, you d'never knaw ... considering whaas expected ov we, this might be my little drill's last dig...

MICHELLE: You want?

JIMMY: 'Course I want ... Dun't you lot be sayin' anything t'Tresawna... This bit ov commerce would be the last straw fur a Methodee like 'ee! After you maid ... Oui... Oui...

MICHELLE *drags* JIMMY *off. Red lighting remains.*

Merge into a sequence where shells land endlessly. With each shell landing, JOHN HENRY *becomes visibly more uncomfortable. At first he scrunches into a ball, and sits there quaking. He covers his ears. His eyes stare forward. Then he gets up and runs around uncontrollably.*

JIMMY *enters, and is surprised to see him reacting in this way.* JIMMY *stops him from running, and presses him down beside him.*

56

JIMMY: Quatty down 'ere with me, my son.

JOHN HENRY: Always ... before ... Jimmy, when I wanted to escape, I could hear the sea, in the west ... the seagulls ... the waves breaking on the shore. And now, I cen't hear a thing.

JIMMY nurses and cradles JOHN HENRY as the bombardment continues. Fade to blackout.

7. A front-line trench, near the Second Battle of Ypres, 22 April, 1915.

Night-time. JOHN HENRY, CHRISTIAAN, JIMMY and WILLIAM are getting ready for an important mission. They each have wire cutters and rifles, or pistols at the ready.

VOICEOVER: Many amongst us are now tired. To those I would say that Victory will belong to the side that holds out the longest. Every position must be held to the last man; there must be no retirement. With our backs to the wall and believing in the justice of our cause each one of us must fight on to the end. The safety and freedom of mankind depends on the conduct of each one of us at this critical moment.

CHRITIAAN: You ready? Just remember all I've taught you.

JIMMY: Ready as I'll ever be.

CHRISTIAAN: Captain Tresawna?

WILLIAM: Time to go.

WILLIAM gestures forward. The group climb the ladder to go over the top of the trench. WILLIAM leads, followed by CHRISTIAAN, and then JIMMY (The need is to go over the sandbags but remain backstage, on a higher level than the stage floor). JOHN HENRY is more reluctant.

JIMMY: You a'right?

JOHN HENRY: Not really ... Not sure I can be doin' ov ut...

JIMMY: Come on pard. Stick with me. I ebm' let 'ee down yet!

JOHN HENRY: I'm ... I'm ... I'm scared Jimmy. I'm really scared. I cen't stop shakin'...

JIMMY: We've 'ad worse in the mine. This is nothun' ... 'Tis just a sap hole in the middle ov a field.

WILLIAM: [*from no man's land*] You two there?

JIMMY: Jus' comin' Cap'n.

JIMMY reaches for JOHN HENRY's hand pulls him up. JIMMY and JOHN HENRY go over the top of the trench.

JIMMY: Aeh, git this over an' we'll soon be a-surfin' back Perran. Think ov tha'...

JOHN HENRY: Yeah. Cen't wait Jimmy. Cen't wait.

JOHN HENRY is still visibly shaking and uncomfortable.

CHRISTIAAN: [*off*] This is the first belt ov ut. Pass me the cutters...

WILLIAM: [*off*] 'Ere... another bundle ... We'll need some bangalores under this lot.

CHRISTIAAN: [*off*] Get down...

JIMMY: [*off*] They 'ent seen us...

WILLIAM: [*off*] Stay low... They'm shinin' torches ... 200 yards...

Torch lights cross no-man's land.

JIMMY: [*off*] I've dun moast ov ut here ... John Henry?

JOHN HENRY: [*off*] Jus' one more section. Double coils though...

CHRISTIAAN: [*off*] Make sure the path's clear ... Where are you Captain?

WILLIAM: [*off*] Down 'ere. Crater to your left.

CHRISTIAN: [*off*] Stay there. They can sense us. I can feel it...

A pause.

JIMMY: [*off*] Whaas' tha' smell?

JOHN HENRY: [*off*] Wha' smell?

JIMMY: [*off*] 'Tidn' me ... Ebm' 'ad onion or turnip fur least a month, you...

CHRISTIAAN: [*off, panicked*] Drop low! I think it's chlorine.

JIMMY: [*off*] Gas!?

CHRISTIAAN: [*off*] Definitely. Pull back. Keep low. Shut your mouths. Crawl into the trench.

Gas (simulated by stage fog) engulfs no man's land; some filtering into the trench and audience. All of them start to cough.

JIMMY: [*off, coughing*] You there ... John Henry....

JOHN HENRY: [*off, spluttering*] Still 'ere.

CHRISTIAAN: [*off, exhaling deeply and painfully*] This ... is the... first time ... they've used it.

JIMMY: [*off, coughing*] Back to the ... trench ... We've masks back there.

A coughing JOHN HENRY *appears at the top of the sand-bags and stumbles, almost falling, into the trench. His coughing continues.* JIMMY *is next in.*

CHRISTIAAN: [*off*] Cover your eyes and mouth.

The gas continues, as does the coughing. CHRISTIAN *enters the trench.*

CHRISTIAAN: It'll disperse. Keep down still.

JOHN HENRY: Where's Cap'n? 'Ee idn' back yet.

They look around for him.

CHRISTIAAN: He's still out there.

JIMMY: I'll go.

JIMMY *stanks up the ladder; a man on a mission.* CHRISTIAAN *tries to stop him.*

CHRISTIAAN: It'll burn your lungs. It'll be too strong ... Leave him. You have to.

JIMMY: We 'ent leavin' ov un ... 'Ee didn' leave me an' I ent leavin' un now.

A crunch of shells start to fall, symbolised by red lights. JOHN HENRY *cowers.* CHRISTIAAN *looks over the trench top. The barrage continues. Suddenly, the face of* WILLIAM *drops out of the darkness at the top of the trench.* JIMMY *is behind him.*

JIMMY: [*to Christiaan*] Give me a 'and.

CHRISTIAAN: Where was he?

JIMMY: In the crater still.

JIMMY *and* CHRISTIAAN *lift/drag him awkwardly down the ladder.* WILLIAM *is conscious, but his lungs are clearly filled with chlorine gas.*

JIMMY: Don't put water in 'is eyes. Wipe 'em out.

JOHN HENRY *wipes them out.*

CHRISTIAAN: He needs air into his lungs.

JIMMY: 'Ere, I 'ent kissin' 'ee...

CHRISTIAAN: It's not forbidden. It's called the Biblical method. You know, like Elihsa and the Shunammite woman's son...

JIMMY: Bleddy Methodee...

JIMMY *gives resuscitation.* WILLIAM *wakes and bursts into a fit of coughing, spewing yellow liquid from his lungs.*

CHRISTIAAN: That's good. If he's coughing.

JIMMY: Cap'n – you'm a'right.

The gas gradually subsides. All of them lower their masks, and bandage WILLIAM'*s eyes.*

CHRISTIAAN: Get him to the field hospital. They'll sort him out.

JOHN HENRY *assists* WILLIAM. WILLIAM *walks out, with his eyes bandaged; his left hand on* JOHN HENRY'*s shoulder.*

JIMMY: Will a be a'right ... really?

CHRISTIAAN: Some scarring on the lungs I expect.

WILLIAM: [*shouting back*] You there Jimmy?

JIMMY: 'Ere ... Cap'n.

WILLIAM: I was wrong 'bout you Tamblyn, wudn't I?

JIMMY: Not wrong ... You dun' me right, an' I did you right. By my reck'n-ing, we'm quits.

WILLIAM: Quits 'tis then...

WILLIAM *holds out his hand for* JIMMY *to shake.* JIMMY *finds it.* CHRISTIAAN *and* JOHN HENRY *lead off* WILLIAM. JIMMY *is left on his own. A bounce on the lights.*

It is a few minutes later. JIMMY *is gazing at his gas mask. He coughs. The enormity of what has just occurred begins to show.*

JIMMY: [*logically, to himself*] Never thought this day would come – quits with Tresawna ... 'Ee edn' got nothun on me no more ... Not now ... [*pause, smiles to himself*] You never knaw. Might even get me job back mine...

ROBERT WALLING *enters, with a gas mask on. He looks like an alien, and speaks incomprehensibly, almost comically, from inside the mask.* JIMMY *points to his own face.*

JIMMY: Take yer mask off Mr Walling!

WALLING *looks blank at the audience, still with the mask on.*

JIMMY: Is' safe! The gas 'ent here no more...

WALLING: Can I take it off?

JIMMY: [*annoyed*] Now, would I be here like this if twudn' a'right?

WALLING *nods. He takes off the mask.*

WALLING: It's late. We should...

JIMMY: I know. But...

WALLING: Tresawna?

JIMMY: Yeah – Christiaan reckons 'ee'll survive ... Gibm' time an' 'ee'll be back 'ere bossing we round.

WALLING: Go down, this will. The first time the Germans used gas. It isn't just here. It's all along the front ... A good story to send back. Show the Boche for what they are.

JIMMY: Right.

WALLING *sits next to* JIMMY. *A pause.*

WALLING: What was it like Jimmy? Over the top I mean...

JIMMY: [*yawning*] Proper 'ellish, you.

WALLING: Describe it for me.

JIMMY: I 'ent no writer like you, Mr Walling...

A pause.

JIMMY: [*thoughtful*]. Well, I d'knaw land. I've known land all my life. Dug inta whacks of ut. But this lot, well, this 'ere no man's land ... 'tis like I imagine hell t'be. Like how they describe ut back chapel. I dunnaw what more t'say ... 'Tis like I've lost me tongue ... No words t'describe ut...

Darkness starts to engulf the stage.

WALLING : [*muttering darkly*] Bes dên heb tavaz a gollas e dîr.

JIMMY: What 'ee say?

WALLING: Nothing ... Something I've learned ... Just reminded me – that's all ... a proverb: A man without a tongue lost his land. We mustn't lose it...

JIMMY: What, the tongue you mean?

WALLING: No. [*beat*] Damn the tongue. I'm talking about No Man's Land. Too many souls gone to let it go now ... Sometimes, Jimmy, it's hard to know what to write. How can I serve the Empire and write propaganda for back home, when there's nothing positive to say?

JIMMY: That I dunnaw.

Pause. WALLING *puts his head in his hands.*

JIMMY: Come on, Mr Walling, let me fix 'ee a rum. You d'look like you need one.

A blackout. The lights flip to a bright summer morning.

8. A Trench System, near the Somme, 29 June, 1915.

JIMMY *is singing badly. He finds* WALLING *sat near the box, absurdly colouring in with pastels, fastidiously, but neatly. On stage left,* JOHN HENRY *is on his own, cleaning his weapon.*

JIMMY: [*singing*]

The world wudn' made in a day.
And Eve didn' ride on a bus.
But most of the world's in a sandbag.
And the rest of it's splattered on us.

Listen, John Henry, I got grub an' niceys 'ere. Bully beef, biscuits, margarine, plum jam, tea an' cocoa. Drop ov rum too. A right Johnny Fortnight, me.

There is no reaction from JOHN HENRY. *He is distant and separate.*

62

JIMMY: An' I've been fumigated good an' proper. No lice on me! Tell 'ee wha' though – this bleddy trench foot. It d'draw yer feet some. June an' es damper an' colder here than back in the mine bottoms, an' then we'm lagged with mud. [*beat*] A'right Mr Walling. What 'ee doin' ov?

WALLING: It's a magazine.

JIMMY: You'm writin' a magazine. What here in the trenches! Show me ... Look at this John Henry. Mr Walling 'ere got a magazine goin'.

JOHN HENRY *does not respond*. WALLING *shows him*.

WALLING: Here, look.

JIMMY: Whaas this written in? Cornish again be ut? You an your Cornish. Gaa – waaste ov time. You knaw no bugger d'speak it no more dun-nee'? An' I thought you said...

JIMMY *stops*.

WALLING : I speak it.

JIMMY: Like I said to you back mine, cen't see much point enet meself... an' 'specially out 'ere. Whaas the title ov ut?

WALLING: *An Houlsedhas*. The West – see the sunset over the cliffs. It reminds me of home. See there, *Penskrivennias*: that means editor.

JIMMY: 'Es, an' your name on ut. How d'ee do ut?

WALLING: I had some paper. I hand-coloured it with pastels. In the dug-out at night ... by the light of one of your sticking tommies. Ends the boredom between attacks.

JIMMY: Whyfore?

WALLING: To see if it's possible. I sent the first one back home to Mr Jenner – the foremost expert.

JIMMY: Did a like ut?

WALLING: Yes. He wrote back to me. Said how this was just the sort of thing we needed. He was amazed I had sent it from here. He thinks it could really help Cornish recover. A new surge, eh?

Beat.

JIMMY: I still think you'm a bit maazed in the 'ead. [*giving Robert a shove*] You should have come with me inta St Omer ... This maid there,

Michelle, she 'ad buddles like...

JIMMY *makes the shape of her breasts, but senses* WALLING *is not interested.*

JIMMY: [*trying another tack*] Have you stopped writing for the Mercury then, Mr Walling?

Jimmy is still flicking through 'An Houlsedhas'.

WALLING: It seems ... I've run out of words too, Jimmy. In one language, at least. Like you ... when you told me ... All that we've seen and been through. All this horror. I've no more words t'describe it. In English, at least.

JIMMY: Maybe ... boy ... maybe ... Whaas this? A keenly drawing.

WALLING: It's a tank. I wrote a description of it in Cornish ... They're bringing them up to the front on trains ... Should help end this stupid war of attrition.

JIMMY: Dun't 'spect anyone else've done that before. Read ut to me.

WALLING: An "Tank", neb-yu man gerûsga kalés, yu ingwin a vresul ancouth. Pan an Almannion a'n welas an kensa gwéth therons î neseas, orestumyuner rag ouni kez ... [*Translation: The tank is a hard vehicle which is a strange machine for warfare. When the Germans saw it for the first time they were confused, and overwhelmed with fear.*]

His words sound utterly poetic, and take both men back to Cornwall. As WALLING *comes to the end of his sentences, there is a loud crump of a 77mm Field Gun shell landing close by. The stage darkens and red light symbolises the explosions.*

JIMMY: C-hr-ist. That wuz a big bugger! They Germans didn't like that what you'd written about that tank ...

WALLING: Close by too...

JIMMY: Come on, Mr Walling, into the dug out. They there Boche whizzbangs'll be 'itting 'ere soon enough.

Further shells land. WALLING *and* JIMMY *run to the dug-out, but* JOHN HENRY *does not move. The shells land with even more power.* JIMMY *and* WALLING *are forced to take further cover.*

The focus turns to JOHN HENRY. *The red light continues, and the shelling is obviously continuing. The sound of the shells is replaced by Euphoria trance music.* JOHN HENRY *drops his weapon. He stands up and moves closer to the audience. He gets undressed, discarding his helmet and jacket, so that he stands in only his vest and trousers. His face betrays a psychological scarring that is unrecoverable. He gives one last look back to the dug-out in which are huddled* JIMMY *and* WALLING, *but he has already made up his mind to desert. He deserts and leaves the stage. The Euphoria music fades, so the shell-fire continues. This continues for a few seconds then the stage becomes black.* WALLING *and* JIMMY *leave through the back of the dug-out.*

Flip the light to full brightness suddenly. We see a self-harming JOHN HENRY *sat on the floor, rocking, obviously alone, scared and damaged. He weeps uncontrollably.*

9. A Trench System, near the Somme, 1 July, 1915.

In semi-darkness, WILLIAM *and* JIMMY *after the Ypres gas attack, now closer are sat drinking a brew and playing cards.* WALLING *enters.*

WALLING: They've found him. Ten miles back. In woodland. He'd made a fire. Some children spotted him. Every limb was shaking. They said he wouldn't speak.

JIMMY: [*cynical*] Couldn' speak more like...

WALLING : They had to tie him down to a stretcher. It's that battle nervousness I believe.

WILLIAM: Tell the authorities to bring him up to the Front here. He'll be put before the military court, for desertion. What do they say – *Pour encourager les autres*...

JIMMY: [*head in his hands*] No ... Dun't they knaw 'ee idn' even legal ... The British army. Your country needs you, but if you 'ent well, then we court martial 'ee...

WALLING: It's obvious. The lad had had enough, and took flight. There's a new word for it: shellshock. That's it. Can't you see that, Captain?

WILLIAM: 'Course I see it. It's not for me t'say. It's out of my hands.

WALLING: With all due respect, he's one of us ... You can stop this now. Protest ... Say what a brave fellow he has been. Tell the Colonel or something ... Surely what is needed is an appropriate response to the

65

circumstances of Private Pascoe's conditions instead of slavishly adhering to the rules? Just how am I meant to report this incident Captain?

WILLIAM: It's over my head Mr Walling. If one gets away with it, we'd have no army. John Henery'll have to accept his fate.

WALLING : That what you been told to say is it? *Bes dên heb tavaz a gollas e dîr.*

WILLIAM *ignores him and goes back to playing cards. Utterly depressed,* JIMMY *has scattered the pack.*

JIMMY: 'Es – you've served un some rough.

JIMMY *leaves with* WALLING. WILLIAM *is left on his own; his winning hand utterly useless.*

10. A Communications Trench, near the Somme, 3 July, 1915.

Dawn. A handcuffed JOHN HENRY *is marched on stage by* WILLIAM TRESAWNA, *who is carrying a blanket and blindfolding materials. He is led to an execution post (a shell-destroyed tree), and tied there. An unwilling* JIMMY *marches in, holding a rifle. Project further members of the firing squad.* WALLING *enters as an observer, taking notes as the execution proceeds.*

WILLIAM: [*as he blindfolds John Henry*] You didn' follow the rules. Rules is everything in my book. Rules is everything in the army's book too. There's nothun' I could do.

WILLIAM *turns away from* JOHN HENRY.

WILLIAM: Call in the men.

The sound of a seagull, who has come in from the sea. As the VOICEOVER *is read,* JIMMY *enters as the firing squad.*

VOICE: [*off*] Private No. 2120 John Henry Pascoe, Duke of Cornwall's Light Infantry, has been charged and found guilty of when on active service, of shamefully abandoning post in the presence of the enemy. He has been convicted and sentenced to death. This sentence has been confirmed by Field Marshal Sir John French, Commander-in-Chief, British Expeditionary Force, and will be carried out at dawn on 3rd July 1915.

WILLIAM *nods at the firing squad. He raises a white hankerchief. This is the cue for the firing squad to charge their rifles.*

JIMMY: [*unable to help himself, weeping*] Sure you wun't'do this Tresawna?

JOHN HENRY: [*to himself, quietly*]

And shall Trelawny live?
And shall Trelawny die?
Here's twenty thousand Cornish men
Will know the reason why!

William lowers his handkerchief.

The sound of rifle fire, and its echo. For a second, JOHN HENRY's *body barely moves, then the head drops. On top of the excavation shaft, the* GIRL *looks on. A projection of waves. From this unreal moment, pull back to reality.* JIMMY *can barely believe what has passed.* WILLIAM *unties the body, which falls to the floor. He bends to check* JOHN HENRY *is dead, showing no emotion. The* GIRL *leaves.*

WILLIAM: Use the blanket.

A sobbing JIMMY *crosses the stage and transfer* JOHN HENRY's *body onto the blanket.*

WILLIAM: [*still strong*] Bury the body will you? In the next field.

JIMMY: Pards to the end, eh? I'll dig fur 'ee boy – one last time.

JIMMY exits dragging JOHN HENRY's *body behind him.* WILLIAM *is left on his own. At first, there is not discernable change in his countenance. Then slowly, his whole body crumples.* JIMMY *enters, aggressive.*

JIMMY: Try tellin' Mrs Pasca' about the Law eh ... Or that dear maid ov 'is ... That the plan 'ere es ut? Not enough killin' goin' on by the enemy fur 'ee? So you 'ave t'kill your own boys, eh? S'pause it'll all be dressed up as somethun' or nothun' – missing in action or somethun'...

WILLIAM *turns to him.*

WILLIAM: Tamblyn, what am I goin' t'do?

JIMMY tries to answer but he cannot. He is tongueless again. JIMMY *opens his arms, and comforts* WILLIAM. WALLING *speaks as he takes notes.* JIMMY *looks at him.*

ROBERT: For dispatches ... The world must know the truth ... This how they treat shellshock is it? I've done some digging. It's a medical condition. More and more of the correspondents are writing about it. People must know...

The way JIMMY *looks at him makes* WALLING *stop writing.*

JIMMY: Perhaps not...

A pause.

WALLING: [*agreeing*] Perhaps not.

WALLING *nods, ripping the page from his notebook, scrunching it into a tight ball. He knows that what he is witnessing is too terrible to share.* WALLING *walks off.* JIMMY *comforts a sobbing* WILLIAM. *The lights fade to black. Music: 'Hail to the Homeland'.*

Act Three

1. Abandoned North Wheal Leisure Mine, Perranporth, Cornwall, at the start of the twenty-first century.

MAISIE *enters, by sitting on top of the trench. She is wearing a surf dress and sandals. She is on a mobile, and sips from a can of Diet Coke.*

MAISIE: Okay. Pick me up at ten. [*pause*] Yeah, I'll be ready. [*beat*] I'm all packed. [*beat*] Later! [*to audience*] We're goin' travellin'. Yeah – this lad I'm seeing. Kairn right? He's bought a camper, an' so we thought we'd head over to France – surfin' off Brittany, then heading down to La Graviere ... Everyone says there's some fast tubes down there. Uni's over thank God. Eh, I got a first for that project. Yeah – surprised meself there I can tell you. I found out about these guys, right, from Perranporth. They were out in Flanders, an' one of them got shell shock see, an' he deserted. So I researched it. Then, they called it NYDN. Not Yet Diagnosed Neurosis. What's up with that? Now they know what it is. They call it Post Traumatic Stress Disorder. I mean now, they know how to treat it ... Back then, they didn't have a clue. An' guess what, the ones comin' back from Afghanistan and Iraq, they're coming down here, to surf ... to help them recover. Can you believe tha'? Surfing soldiers [*laughs*]. But the cool thing, was this one lad ... He was only fifteen ... I reckon he was in my family ... only they left him off the memorial didn' they? No poppies for him in November. I'm gonna' change that ... when I get back. Thaas a definite. So I'm getting' into me history you could say. There's all these layers of time right ... I was thinkin' about ut. St Piran. 'Ee comed in on the surf too ... Yeah, kicked out of Ireland, but Cornwall's first surfer. Cool. I'n see ut now – a stonking long board in the seventh century! [*her mobile vibrates*]. Excuse me. Thaas him again ... [*looks at mobile*] 'Ee's just left Plymouth. Right, I'd best be off. Laters...

2. A shaft, North Wheal Leisure Mine, Perranporth, Cornwall, 31 July, 1918.

The sound of rainfall. JIMMY *and* WILLIAM *step onto the shaft and gaze into mid-distance. Both hold their collars close to their necks.*

WILLIAM: But that's what the Military want.

JIMMY: I cud see what they wuz spellin' out fur'n, and wha', not tell everyone back here?

WILLIAM: Rose d'knaw. You told the maid?

JIMMY: I see'd her. She knaws. I'm not sure 'ow. Sensed ut I think.

WILLIAM: They need to know. I don't care about anyone else.

JIMMY: Whaas the official line then?

WILLIAM: Killed in action.

JIMMY: But the Memorial that's planned for the Square?

WILLIAM: His name wun't go on ut. They won't have it. No deserters to be recognised. Not just here, but right the way cross the country...

JIMMY: Why dun' 'um just tell the truth Cap'n?

WILLIAM: The truth? [*pause*] Jimmy, I dun't think there is any truth any more.

WILLIAM *exits.* JIMMY *jumps down to the shaft, and, almost for devilment, lights a sticking tommy. He then exits.*

3. The kitchen of the Pascoe household, Pencrennow Farm, 7 August, 1918.

The sound of rainfall. The door opens. A rain-socked ROSE PASCOE *enters, with a clothes basket, filled with items she has just taken off the line.*

ROSE: [*stoically*] Weather idn' ut? 'Ot this mornin' – but it've comed in wet. I'd just put the clothes out too. 'Twas close too, that day. I remember. It rained in the late afternoon. I wudn' 'ome when the telegram comed. I was out walkin' down beach. I dun't knaw why. They come to find me. Mrs Pasca' – a man here from the Telegraphy. You dun't need tellun'. You know already. You can feel ut. There was somethun' a few days before. I was in the kitchen, an' I could feel him in pain somewhere. Hurtin' bad. A mother can feel tha'. I'd nearly

70

walked the length of the beach, and before the rain comed in, it was one of they summer dogs' days. In winter, when 'tis cold, y'dream ov days like that ... but not that day. An' when they told me, I was back mine ten years before when Archie went on. The same 'ole in your 'eart that grows an' grows. It eats away at 'ee. At night. When you're alone.

ROSE *begins folding up and piling the washing as she talks.*

ROSE: [*matter of factly*] An' the pity that do go with ut. People do avoid 'ee, like they'm afraid ov 'ee, when you need they moast. I knaw why. It's cuz they'm scared t'say the wrong thing. So I thanked the man from Telegraphy. "Thank you," I said, and I was down on the beach. There wudn' a soul there, from up Penhale t'Droskyn. An' I knew what I 'ad to do. I 'ad to go up Garnbargus and tell the maid. Close an' sticky that day. I wuz blawed time I got there. She was out bringin' in the cows fur milking. A lot of flies, I knaw tha'. An' the cows – all beautiful, dark, loving eyes and slobber, as they comed down off the moor. All fulla' bussy milk fur their calves. She didn' need tellun' neither. Just by me being there – turnin' up out of the blue – she knew. An' 'er face, dear ov 'er. Pain went into ut that day. All she cud do wuz sit down and cry, an' the cows comed down, an' circled us. An' when we sobbed together, we scared them a bit ... An' as we held each other, then ut started t'rain ... so we'm sat there, holding each other, in the mud.

A knock at the door disturbs her thoughts. ROSE *answers it. It is a rain-soaked* WILLIAM TRESAWNA.

WILLIAM: Rose...

ROSE: Cap'n Tresawna.

William removes his bowler hat, nervously holding it with both hands at waist height. The following is filled with unspoken tension.

WILLIAM: Can I have a word?

ROSE: S'many as y'like.

WILLIAM: About John Henery.

ROSE: [*hard*] What else? What about un?

WILLIAM: You knaw what 'appened, dun't 'ee?

ROSE: Mr Walling told me. When a told me, I was up ninety.

WILLIAM: It was unavoidable. He...

ROSE: I knaw. He deserted. Runned off like a coward. We ebm' told no one.

WILLIAM: If it hadn't been me, it'd have been someone else.

ROSE: I understand Cap'n Tresawna. The law is the law. What would ut be like if we all broke the law?

WILLIAM *doesn't answer.*

ROSE: Aside from tha', wuz a good an' brave over there?

WILLIAM: 'Ee was a brave man Rose.

ROSE: Man? Barely a man by my reckoning. Then thaas 'is stupid fault...

WILLIAM: A brave lad then ... Braver than many men.

ROSE: Say that – will ut? On his gravestone? Not on the Memorial either, from what I gather.

WILLIAM: No.

ROSE: In a field wudn' ut? Was 'is grave even marked?

ROSE *folds the clothes more vigorously, taking her anger out on them.*

WILLIAM: Yes. A cross, and his name, of course.

ROSE: Minister there, wuz there?

WILLIAM: Yes. A padre.

Beat.

ROSE: Did a call fur me or the maid? [*pause*] Hardly ever wrote y'knaw ... That's John Henry fur 'ee. Like 'is faather. Never much good with pen and paper. Better with pick-axe and pump.

WILLIAM *stands close to her.*

WILLIAM: Rose, he called for you ... We talked a lot before ... He told me to write those letters to you.

ROSE: Before 'ee got the nervousness?

WILLIAM: Yes, in trainin'. At Mons. In Flanders.

ROSE: What a say?

WILLIAM: 'Ee said ... he talked 'bout you an' me. He had dreams too.

ROSE: 'Ee wanted t'be you. One day, 'ee wanted your job at mine. Progress there like. Work 'is way up.

WILLIAM: I know ... I do know.

WILLIAM *turns away.*

ROSE: What' am I meant to say to 'is maid? She been some good t'me y'knaw.

WILLIAM: I'll talk to her. I know Jimmy's tried.

ROSE: Talkin' wun't being un back though will ut William? [*mad now with anger*] 'Ee's gone on – not like you an' Jimmy, and the rest ov um. That idn' the way 'tis meant t'be. [*pause*] Jimmy's cut up 'bout ut. Did 'ee pull the trigger then?

WILLIAM: 'Ee wuz one of many. Twelve men. They formed a squad.

ROSE: Cudn' 'ee have stopped um?

WILLIAM: Jimmy?! Jimmy didn' 'ave no choice neither. Sometimes the choice is no choice Rose. Would you have 'ad them shoot low an' 'ee die in agony?

ROSE: Cap'n Tresawna, every day since 'ee left fur France, I been chapel, and prayed an' prayed, but ebm' dun no good 'ave ut? You knaw – you bein' a religious man. I dun't think the Lord be lookin' after me. I be teared up t'lerrups over ut.

WILLIAM: Dun't say that.

ROSE: I'm goin' t'say ut. Since the telegram I ebm' been back there. I shen't be goin' again neither.

WILLIAM: 'Ave the Minister been to see 'ee?

ROSE: 'Aw 'es. Just like las' time. Even got that Reverend Hockin' t'come an' have a word. Very nice an' that ... Gived me a book ov faith. I told un me faith in the world 'ave gone. There...

WILLIAM *runs his fingers through his hair.*

WILLIAM: Then have faith in me Rose.

ROSE: In you?

WILLIAM: In me.

ROSE: But you.

WILLIAM: I've always been there for you Rose, an' I will be in the future…

ROSE: But you. You killed my son.

> ROSE *slaps* WILLIAM *in the face and beats her fists into his chest, sobbing. Eventually the attack stops, and* WILLIAM *cradles her.* WILLIAM *kisses her gently on the forehead to comfort her, and when she looks up, their eyes meet, and they rage into a kiss. Neither can quite believe what has transpired. The lights darken.*

4. Polmassick's funeral directors and carpentry workshop, Perranporth, 20 September, 1918.

> POLMASSICK *is working in the shop, measuring two lengths of 2x4, which he is about to cut. Next to him is a carpenter's bag, and several of the tools inside are used during the conversation which ensues.* POLMASSICK *walks with a limp (the result of a mining accident), obviously unable to have served during the conflict. After the measuring,* POLMASSICK *stands there scratching his head, not quite sure what to do.* JIMMY *enters.*

JIMMY: [*less ebullient than before*] Since when've you moved inta' the profitable world of death then, eh? Coffins and carpentry. [*joking*] Better than they damn durns you fitted backalong over mine.

> *Polmassick turns around to see* JIMMY. *They shake hands.*

POLMASSICK: Jimmy boy, how be 'ee? Adjustin' t'life back 'ome are 'ee? [*changing tone*] Eh – some wisht 'bout boy Pasca'…

> JIMMY *does a sharp intake of breath.*

JIMMY: Wisht…

POLMASSICK: You there was 'ee?

JIMMY: When?

POLMASSICK: When a died.

JIMMY: 'Es, I wuz … Seen ut 'appen … so t'speak.

POLMASSICK: I cudn' 'ave stomached ut Jimmy. Not by what the Mercury do say ov ut. Hell on earth they reckon. Like that wuz ut?

JIMMY: 'Es. Just like tha'. Thaas' 'zactly what 'twas like.

POLMASSICK: Shakin' up three million dead over there, they d'say.

JIMMY: 'Es, keep you in good business 'Massick. So ... how's mine goin' on?

POLMASSICK: 'Tidn goin' on t'all. No call fur tin now the war's over. What 'ee think I'm doin' up 'ere? No choice but t'work with faathur again see: bit ov schemey with wood an' burials....

JIMMY: [in reflective mood] 'Es, well, like I say, there's good money in death. Mine shut then es ut?

POLMASSICK: Nawbody got sense ov ut see. Least Tresawna knawed what t'do. 'Ee idn' no ordinary fool. Maybe now 'ee's back, 'twill start up again. [beat] You an' 'ee still...?

JIMMY: 'Es, still at ut, like armies on the West'n Front. Maybe a bit closer though. War do that to men.

POLMASSICK: 'Es, I 'spect so.

JIMMY: So no more North Wheal Leisure?

POLMASSICK: I dunnaw boy. I'll be 'onest with 'ee. I cen't see much ov a future fur ut. The best years ov ut is behind we.

JIMMY: You'm right there... [beat] Listen, I need a favour...

POLMASSICK: I'm listenin'.

JIMMY: I d'want some wood, see. Only I want ut made inta this shape...

JIMMY *unfurls a piece of paper from his pocket, and shows him the drawing on it.* POLMASSICK *scratches his head.*

POLMASSICK: That shape? That size? Whyfore?

JIMMY: Got a bit of an idea out ov coor.

POLMASSICK: Tell 'ee wha'. I knaw wha' your best bet is fur tha'. Come back 'ere with me. Got a passel ov they you'n 'ave.

POLMASSICK *and* JIMMY *exit.*

5. Shaft No. 6 at North Wheal Leisure Mine, Perranporth, 12 October, 1918.

The sound of a seagull overhead. The GIRL *is sat on the shaft, positioned just like* MAISIE *at the start of the play.* JIMMY *enters below.*

JIMMY: You'm lookin' like a winnard.

GIRL: What do you want?

JIMMY: To talk some more. To tell 'ee the truth.

GIRL: The truth?

JIMMY: Yeah.

GIRL: You was supposed t'be 'is pard...

JIMMY: I was. I still am.

GIRL: [*angry*] That why he be 'ere right now es ut?

The GIRL *looks away from* JIMMY.

JIMMY: 'Ee wudn' killed in action. 'Ee deserted. I cen't put ut any other way. One minute 'ee was there, an the next, 'ee wudn'. Out there, military law dun't take no prisoners. Desert, an' you'm shot.

GIRL: [*beat*] I need t'knaw. Who gave orders for his death?

JIMMY: The field court. Generals. The bettermoast sort. Y'knaw: English-types, with cushy digs behind the lines. Toffs. Big wigs with canes.

GIRL: No. Who gived the actual order? [*pause*] Mr Walling said ut wuz Tresawna.

JIMMY: Mr Walling tell 'ee?

GIRL: 'Ee come to see me ... and Mrs Pasca'. 'Ee said 'ee was going t'write 'bout ut – but then 'ee changed is mind. Thought the better ov ut I believe. Said ut wudn' do anybody no good.

JIMMY: If you knaw, then I'll go. There's no more t'say.

The GIRL *jumps down to* JIMMY's *level.*

GIRL: [*powerful*] No. I need to knaw. Answer me. Was 'ee a hero Jimmy? I mean, just tell me ... Tell me somethun' 'ee dun good.

JIMMY: [*thinking*] John Henry could crawl in spaces I could never fit inta.

At the excavations in Mons, before we retreated, the mines 'ee fixed saved 'undreds ov our boys. That good enough fur 'ee.

GIRL: 'Ee never wrote t'me you knaw.

JIMMY: 'Ee wanted t'spare you.

GIRL: Spare me?

JIMMY *reaches out to hold her by the shoulders.*

JIMMY: Maid, 'ee loved you. I d'knaw tha'. 'Ee loved you in a way I can only ever wish fur. [*aside*] All I 'ave is blowsy maids in Flanders, or back Bolingey. [*beat*] Moast people never ever touch tha'. Never get tha' far.

Unexpectedly, JIMMY *produces an object from his pocket.*

JIMMY: 'Ere, 'ee made you this.

GIRL: What is ut?

JIMMY: A bit ov' art. Good edn' ut? From a shell casing. You do ut when you'm waitin' hours on end fur the whistle to go ... Is' a copper heart see...

GIRL: A heart?

Jimmy hands the heart to the GIRL.

JIMMY: Maid, you wuz always in his heart. 'Ee wuz terrible 'bout 'ee. Always remember tha'. Remembrance, yeah – fur the future...

JIMMY *begins to leave.*

GIRL: [*softer*] Jimmy ... Sorry ... I never thought much ov you ... in the past, I mean.

JIMMY: Not many people do.

GIRL: I knaw different now.

JIMMY: Dun't tell naw bugger. They'll ave me stroathin' down Chapel, and staying 'ome from the Wink. I'll be on Temperance marches next...

Beat.

GIRL: You were in the firin' squad wunnee'?

JIMMY: I wuz. 'Ad orders. 'Ad to. Just like Tresawna.

GIRL: What wuz ut like?

JIMMY: [*dreamily*] 'Tis 'ard t'call un 'ome now ... but when I wuz standin' there, I wuz thinkin' ov how me an' John 'Enry 'ad this idea ... You'll see. We wanted t'ride the waves. We made a pact together.

GIRL: Wha' the surf?

JIMMY *turns to her.*

JIMMY: The white horses yeah. The ones ol' St Piran comed in on.

GIRL: How?

JIMMY: Come down beach, this Saturday. I'll shaw 'ee.

GIRL: I cen't go there now. It reminds me...

JIMMY: The dunes then? Watch ut from up there. I've invited Mr Walling. The Mercury's goin' t'carry a feature on ut.

GIRL: A'right. I'll be there.

JIMMY: See you then ... Keep faith an' soul maid.

JIMMY *moves to leave.*

GIRL: Jimmy?

JIMMY *stops.*

GIRL: The firin' squad...?

JIMMY: I 'ad to. If I didn', well ... someone else would've had to. [*pause*] I closed me eyes, fired, an' then 'ee wuz gone.

The GIRL *nods, then smiles.* JIMMY *smiles and leaves. Alone, the* GIRL *holds up the copper heart, and presses it to her own. The lights dim. She exits. A projection of waves breaking on the shore.*

6. The 'Western Daily Mercury' newspaper office, Plymouth 8 November, 1918.

Night-time. The dull light of a newspaper office. A table on top of which is a heavy, large iron typewriter. MRS SLATTERY *enters carrying a cup and saucer.*

MRS SLATTERY: [*respectful, but still deferential*] Mr Walling? Would you like your tea now? I'll bring it in for you if you like.

WALLING: [off] No, I'll be out Mrs Slattery. [yawns] Could do with stretching my legs.

A newly-promoted WALLING *enters through the door. He blows on the cup to cool it, then takes a sip of tea.*

MRS SLATTERY: So how has your day been?

WALLING: What – first day in the saddle? Alright I think...

MRS SLATTERY: Mr Higgins would have wanted you to take over ... He had a lot of faith in you, you know, Mr Walling.

WALLING: That why he sent me to Flanders?

MRS SLATTERY: Come on Mr Walling, you were chomping at the bit. You virtually had your kit-bag packed.

WALLING: I thought it would be different. I'm just grateful to be back in one piece.

MRS SLATTERY: I've noticed that you don't say very much about it.

WALLING: What's there to say? It's all been said. I'm tongue-tied. I've no eloquence anymore. I can hardly write my name these days. Eveyone's built up cliché upon cliché, like sandbags in a trench. Colossal waste of lives. The Great War. *An Bressel Mear!* War to end all wars.

MRS SLATTERY: And will it?

WALLING : I very much doubt it. Humanity functions on greed. Greed always leads to one nation trying to take over another – and those without voices, without tongues, always losing. The way of the world. This century'll have a glut of it.

MRS SLATTERY: I suppose so. Did you hear? The Allied War council have accepted the German armistice terms.

WALLING: We'll see what comes down the wire, though I'll be doing a piece on Perranporth ... for Monday's edition.

MRS SLATTERY: Again? More Cornish tomfoolery Mr Walling? [pause] How's that girl? The one who...

WALLING: Remarkably well, considering...

MRS SLATTERY: And that bull-headed Tresawna, the captain of the mine?

WALLING: That's the thing. He told me. He's asked Mrs Pascoe to marry him.

MRS SLATTERY: Well, what a story – after what happened. You are going to write that up aren't you?

WALLING: I've no interest in tittle-tattle. That's not the story. [*beat*] I promised them – back in Flanders – not to do anything ... Some things are best left unsaid. Not for the public domain.

MRS SLATTERY: So what is?

WALLING: You'll see Mrs Slattery. Something that the world needs to see, more than ever.

Blackout. Euphoria music merging into 'Hail the Homeland'.

7. Perran Sands, facing the Atlantic Ocean, 10 November, 1918.

JIMMY and WILLIAM stand next to ROBERT WALLING. The GIRL is in front of WALLING. All of them face the projection of the ocean, with their backs to the audience.

WALLING: In memory of all the young men of Cornwall who lost their lives in the Great War. [*reads*] *A Dhew ollgallosek ha tregeredhus, neb a dhisquedhas dhyn dre sacrifis Dha Unvap an hens dhe vudhygolyeth war beghes ha'n bedh, a leun golon y commendyen dhe'th hwith ha'th cur Jy mebyon an blu ma neb a geskerdhas bys y'n houlsedhas yn myttin aga dedhyow. Gront dhedha a'th torn ollgallosek le ha hanow nefra a bes, ha budhygolyeth war vresel kepar del waynsys Jy budhygolyeth war Ankow y honen. A hemma y'th pysyn yn hanow Dha Unvap agan Arluth Yesu Crist. Amen.*

ALL: Amen.

JIMMY: [*as an aside to* WALLING] Beautiful tha' Mr Walling. Didn' understand a word ov ut – but beautiful all the same.

WALLING : I got Mr Jenner to correct it. I think he approved.

JIMMY: Got a translation 'ave 'ee?

WALLING: And so, in the other tongue: Almighty and merciful God, who didst show us by the sacrifice of Thine only Son the way to victory over sin and the grave, we heartily commend to Thy keeping and care the sons of this parish who marched into the sunset in the morning of their days. Grant them with Thine Almighty hand an everlasting name and place, and victory over war such as Thou didst gain over Death itself. This we ask in the name of Thine only Son Jesus Christ our Lord. Amen

WILLIAM: A prayer for all they gone into the west...

GIRL: 'Ee'd've liked that. I knaw 'ee would.

WALLING: Here, Cap'n Tresawna – a copy for Mrs Pascoe. Please tell her I'm thinking of her. She might not appreciate the Christian message, but perhaps the other sentiments may appeal?

WILLIAM: It will give comfort to her Mr Walling – knowing you wrote this.

WILLIAM *and the* GIRL *still face the ocean.* WALLING *and* JIMMY *turn from them to face the audience.*

WALLING: Here, Jimmy. I want you t'have these.

WALLING *passes* JIMMY *a set of 'An Houlsedhas' magazines.*

JIMMY: Your magazines Mr Walling?

WALLING: A full set. Keep them somewhere safe. For you to remember... beyond trench foot, lice and the infernal mud, eh?

JIMMY: Now what was it you taught me in the dugout?... [broken] *Kimmyas kres... dewheles dhe'n bys... ?*

WALLING: ...arta whare.

JIMMY: ...arta whare.

WALLING: That's it: May peace return to the world again – soon...

JIMMY: Come on, I'll buy 'ee all a beer ... even you, Tresawna...

The GIRL *remains. Project an image of* MAISIE *pointing out with her finger. The* GIRL *reaches with her finger until they touch. Lights down. Music: 'Hail to the Homeland'.*

8. Tywarnhayle Square, Perranporth, 10 November, 1918.

The REVEREND JOSEPH HOCKING *on a podium.* ROSE PASCOE *watching, with her back to the audience, holding a handbag.*

HOCKING: ...And that concludes the list of the fallen from this Parish. In the fullness of time, we shall erect a permanent memorial to all those lost. In my hands, I already have received from one architect, the design of a Celtic cross, which we hope to have in place by next Autumn. We must remember that not one life has been lost in vain in this Holy War. [*pause*] I thank you for you attendance at this afternoon's ceremony ... and bid you a safe trip home.

The imagined community leave, and JOSEPH HOCKING *tidies his notes, and also starts to leave.* ROSE *awkwardly remains, and eventually* HOCKING *notices her.*

HOCKING: Mrs Pascoe ... I didn't expect to see you here, what with...

ROSE: [*interrupting*] I dun't s'pause you did.

HOCKING: It's official you know ... His name won't ... so ...

ROSE: I knawed tha'.

HOCKING: So?

ROSE: Reverend Hocking. I 'ave as much right as any mother or faather t'stand here today. An' thaas wha' I'm doing ov. My son may not officially exist, but 'ee exists in my 'eart.

HOCKING: [*impatiently, exasperated*] I must be going.

ROSE: Reverend, I wanted you to knaw ... William ... Cap'n Tresawna ...well, you needn't worry. There's enough ov the Methodee still inside ov me. 'Tis like this – I've forgived 'un.

Rose – in almost military style – turns right and walks off. HOCKING *is left flabbergasted and alone.*

9. Perranporth Beach, 11 November, 1918.

In blackness, a VOICEOVER.

VOICEOVER: Hostilities will cease 11.00 hours today, November 11th. Troops will stand fast in line reached at that hour which will be reported to Corps HQ. Defensive precautions will be maintained. There will be no intercourse of any description with the enemy.

Lights up. JIMMY *enters, shuffling behind a coffin lid, so we do not see his full body.*

JIMMY: Boy Polmassick dun me proud. What 'ee think? Some board ennet? 'Twas due for Frankie Trudgeon's funeral next week (shakin' up 'undred and four 'ee wuz), but 'Massick reckon ee'n make another one up fur 'ee. In fact, I gotta' job lot ov um back there, in case of...

JIMMY *reveals himself from behind the coffin lid. He is wearing a very tight, one-piece, knee-length, black swimming costume, with orange and blue bands across the middle.*

JIMMY: What 'ee think? Stylish, eh? Had that maid back Bolingey knock ut up fur me. Good on turnip an' teddy, but even better on needle an' thread. In fact, I be thinkin' ov makin' ut a bit more permanent with she, now the war's almost over...

WILLIAM: [*off*] Be with 'ee in a minute. I cen't get me legs in this stupid costume...

JIMMY: [*shouting to off*] Comest thou on Cap'n. Stop pussivantin' around. The water's lovely. Bracing I'd say. Cen't beat the Atlantic on a November's afternoon. Better than the picture house, this!

WILLIAM *enters nervously and self-consciously, wearing a red and white striped, one piece swimming costume, carrying a coffin lid surf-board. The lid has 'Cap'n' daubed on it.*

JIMMY: Eh – lookin' good, Cap.

WILLIAM: I feel stupid.

Beat.

JIMMY: Never mind tha'. Come on – the waves is barrelling in. Three foot and clean. Paddle out with me...

Both of them place their boards down, and start paddling out.

JIMMY: Thaas' ut. You got un. We need t'get out a bit...

WILLIAM: [*worried*] How deep es ut?

JIMMY: Not very ... Dunnee' worry any. 'Tis nowhere near s'deep as the water down the eighty-fathom sump...

WILLIAM: How do I know when t'get up?

JIMMY: You'll sense ut.

WILLIAM: Sense ut?

JIMMY: 'Tis all about the feel.

WILLIAM: The feel?

JIMMY: The rhythm of the ocean. Watch!

Music: Grunge/surf rock. A projection of waves. JIMMY *confidently gets up on his surfboard.* WILLIAM *mounts his board less confidently, but manages to stand. They surf together in a joyous moment.*

JIMMY: Whey-hey! Look Cap'n. I be proper 'angin' ten...

WILLIAM: I'm doin' it Jimmy. See...

JIMMY: Dun't troll yer feet. Keep um on the edge.

The moment JIMMY *shouts this,* WILLIAM *wobbles and falls off into the water.*

JIMMY: Ha! You've wiped out boy ... 'Tis all about the skill see ... An' I got bagfuls of ut! Tell 'ee wha' Cap, this 'ere surfin' d'tickle me up ass...!

At this, JIMMY *also falls off. The two grab their boards and meet, bobbing in the ocean. This requires moving the board to neck height and looking over them.*

JIMMY: So, what 'ee think ov this 'ere skiddering 'cross the sea?

WILLIAM: Wonderful Jimmy. Wonderful...

JIMMY: When I'm out here ... I forget. Just like Christiaan said. [*beat*] Can 'ee forget it all Will?

WILLIAM: I'll never forget it ... None ov ut ... Not ever ... but...

JIMMY: This helps?

WILLIAM: Yes. This helps...

A pause.

JIMMY: This be fur John Henry see. We made a pact. Me out ere, I d'reckon, will put is soul t'rest.

ROBERT WALLING *enters.*

JIMMY: Hey – look who 'tis: Reporter ov the Year. Editor these days 'ee es! [*calling*] A'right Mr Walling? Have a geek at Cap'n 'ere...

WALLING: [*shouting*] You're both mad! Come out. Let me get a photograph.

JIMMY *and* WILLIAM *step out of the sea and form a pose for a classic 'surfers-and-their-boards' style photograph.*

JIMMY: Fur the Mercury?

WALLING: Yeah Jimmy. For the Mercury.

JIMMY: Make sure you get me good side...

JIMMY *forms a pose, holding in his chest and stomach. It doesn't last and he lets it sag.* WALLING *takes the photograph. The photograph is projected onto the screen.*

Jimmy: [*excited*] You comin' in? Come on. Polmassick got plenty more lids ... They're ideal, see...

WALLING: No. Not for me. I think I'm too much of a landlubber.

WILLIAM: What's your headline then? I mean, for this story...

WALLING: Not sure ... Wave-riders perhaps ... or Surfing Tommies maybe.

JIMMY: Eh? Tell 'ee wha'. That's brilliant Cap ... That's it. We'm Surfing Tommies.

WILLIAM: Come on Tamblyn. Let's go over Droskyn. Have a bit of competition. See, who can stay on the longest?

JIMMY: I won the first one.

WILLIAM: Best ov three then?

JIMMY: You'm on. Mr Walling ... You keep score will 'ee?

WALLING: Of course I will. I'll get some more photographs as well.

JIMMY *and* WILLIAM *launch their boards again. Music: Grunge/surf rock.* WALLING *moves around the stage taking more photographs from different angles.* JIMMY *and* WALLING *sometimes surf towards him; sometimes towards the audience. Eventually, he becomes frustrated, and suddenly strips to his white long-johns, heading off-stage and returning with a coffin lid surfboard. He swims out and joins* JIMMY *and* WILLIAM.

JIMMY: Yoh! Mr Walling!

WALLING: Couldn't hold back any longer.

WILLIAM: What's Cornish fur surfing?

WALLING: [*deadpan*] *Pleynia war an scroff....*

WILLIAM: You serious?

WALLING: Yeah ... I'm ready Jimmy. Bring it on!

JIMMY: Your party, let's go fur ut! Look at me pleynia war an scroffin'

The three surf. Gradually, the music alters to 'Hail to the Homeland'. A uniform-clad (but shoeless) JOHN HENRY *enters, holding a coffin lid. He swims out to join them. He stands on his board in unison with the others. All the action pauses. Slowly, the others look at him - but say nothing. Music: Grunge/surf rock. All four now surf, crazily and madly:* WILLIAM *and* JOHN HENRY *stage left;* WALLING *and* JIMMY *stage right.*

10. The Atlantic Ocean, 11 November, 1918.

MAISIE *enters, standing on top of the shaft, wearing a wetsuit, and carrying a modern surfboard. She puts her hand up to her eyes to view the ocean.*

MAISIE: [*to audience*] You a'right? I saw you earlier. Surf's up right?

ALL: Right on maid.

She drops her bag on the shaft and jumps down, with her modern board. Music continues. MAISIE *smiles knowingly, but seemingly oblivious to the past surfers. She swims out. She stands on her board. A moment: all ride the waves together. Use the laser lighting effect, with stage fog as the ocean.*

One by one the characters stop surfing, and swim back, coming to hold their coffins lids vertically, in a semi-circle around the stage. They then leave, first WALLING, *then* JIMMY, *then* WILLIAM *and, finally,* JOHN HENRY. MAISIE *remains. She has stopped surfing and leaves her board close to the audience.*

MAISIE: I did ut ... Went to the British Legion and the Council ... He's one the Government investigated. 306 of them. A post-humous conditional pardon. No longer a pariah ... now, a hero. Got his name put on, didn' I? All bright and shiny, yeah – but it's there now, on the Memorial down Tywarnhayle Square: John Henry Pascoe. Just as ut belonged t'be. There with the others: all they souls who gived their lives for us. All unveiled yeah, last Remembrance Day. [*pause*] I remember it this way though...

From her bag, she has left on the shaft, she brings out a wreath of poppies. Slowly, she walks out to her board, and places the wreath upon it. She mimes pushing the board out. She watches it for a moment, then exits. Lights darken.

JOHN HENRY PASCOE *enters. He looks at the board out at sea and then back at the mine. Some pre-recorded voices from the trenches. The same rifle shots sound – from his death at dawn. He finds his way to the shaft and finds a still-lit sticking tommy. He holds it, then blows it out. Lights fade to black. In the style of a passionate Methodist minister, a* VOICEOVER *reads Psalm 107: 23-26.*

VOICEOVER: They that go down to the sea in ships that do business in great waters: These see the works of the Lord, and his wonders in the deep. For he commandeth, and raiseth the stormy wind, which lifteth up the waves thereof. They mount up to the heavens, they go down to the depths: their soul is melted because of trouble.

– END –

United Nations Educational, Scientific and Cultural Organization World Heritage Site of the Cornwall and West Devon Mining Landscape

UNESCO principles are devoted to presentation and education, which focus on preserving authenticity, accurate representation and cherishing distinctive world cultures under threat from globalisation.

The Cornish Mining World Heritage Site (WHS) Office commissions cultural events and activities as an element of and as a means for communicating the nominated Site's Outstanding Universal Value. Re-affirming Cornish Mining culture as a distinctive globally significant expression of an evolving industrial society is one of the key policy aims in the WHS Management Plan. The distinctiveness of Cornish Mining culture should be celebrated, promoted and propagated. The Cornish Mining WHS is made up of 10 separate areas within Cornwall and West Devon; all former mineral mining districts during the period of interest (1700–1914). These comprise a combination of industrial, public and domestic buildings and related structures and landforms that together create the Cornish Mining landscape. The development of innovative deep mining technology and a distinctive mining culture which was subsequently exported across the world created this amazing landscape. World Heritage Site status recognises the contribution that the people who shaped our landscape made to the development of the modern world and puts parts of Cornwall and West Devon on a par with the Pyramids, Stonehenge and the Great Wall of China in terms of their significance to humanity

World Heritage status recognises that the Cornish mining landscape has meaning and significance for all humanity. It is a place to be cherished by all, created by people whose collective effort and contribution to the world we live in command respect.

The Cornish Mining WHS commissions new works from arts practitioners in order to tell the fascinating stories about the landscape and people who created it in new and exciting ways. Our aim is to give fresh insights into our amazing heritage through performance arts of the highest standard.

To find out more visit www.cornishmining.org.uk

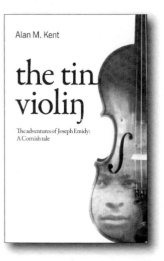
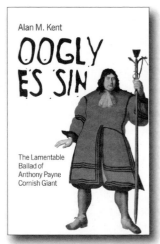
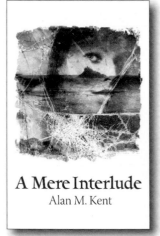
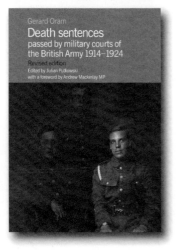

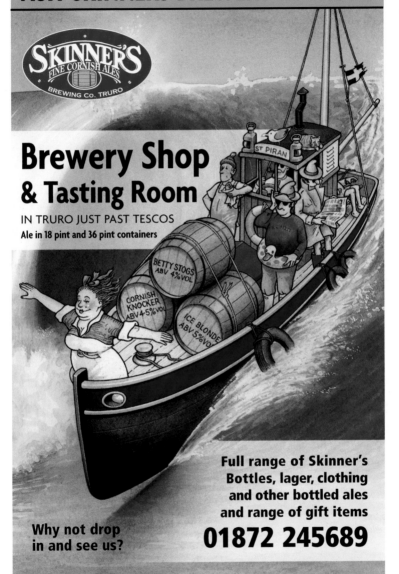

The Hawkins Arms

Fore street, Probus, Truro TR2 4JL Tel. (01726) 882208

Monday–Sunday:
Lunches, 12 noon to 2pm
Evening Meals, 6pm–9pm

Families ALWAYS welcome
Booking not necessary, but advisable

Now open Monday–Saturday at 10am
for Teas, Coffee and Breakfast

Lunches from only £4

THE HOME PUB OF BISHBASHBOSH PRODUCTIONS
Proprietors: Derek and Joan Wills

L. A. NOLAN
& SON

INTERIOR AND EXTERIOR PAINTERS DECORATORS AND HANDYMEN

ARTEXING, COVING, TILING, ETC

FREE ESTIMATES
No Job too Small

TEL: 01726 883004
07977 817363

OUTSTANDING LIVE MUSIC AND LIVE SPORTS BAR

BUNTERS BAR THE BEST VENUE IN CORNWALL FOR...

LIVE MUSIC
WITH TWO STAGE AREAS & WEEKLY MUSIC NIGHTS....

LIVE SPORTS EVENTS
ON 3D TV, BIG SCREEN & 7 PLASMA SCREENS...

WEEKEND DJ
DRINKS PROMOTIONS & A GREAT ATMOSPHERE

PROUD SUPPORTERS OF

BUNTERS BAR
LITTLE CASTLE STREET
TRURO CORNWALL
TR1 3DL
01872241220
WWW.BUNTERSBAR.CO.UK
INFO@BUNTERSBAR.CO.UK

YOU CAN ALSO FIND US ON

SEARCH BUNTERS & B-SIDE AT BUNTERS

The Driftwood Spars

dining · bars · rooms · music · brewery · st agnes cornwall

The ideal base to escape the stresses of modern life and enjoy
the magical vista of the sea, not to mention an award winning
brewery and locally sourced menu

www.driftwoodspars.co.uk

Penrose House

Serviced Apartments

Redruth ● Cornwall

Serviced apartments are different from most types of accommodation you'll find in Cornwall...

Each of our apartments are stylish and functional and ready to receive up to four guests. We take care of all your basic needs, providing you with your own self-contained apartment where you can come and go as you like.

Penrose apartments are available at last minute for stays of any duration. Whether you're visiting for a family holiday, a cosy weekend break or a business meeting, our apartments will be the perfect base from which you will enjoy your Cornish experience.

To find out how we can make your visit to Cornwall truly memorable send us a message-
post@penroseapartments.co.uk
Or call-
01209 218294 / 07840420740

Stuart Chapman

Builder & roofing contractor

Dorsam House, Fore Street,
Probus, Truro TR2 4NB

01726 882 952
07967 809 785

Registered House Builder

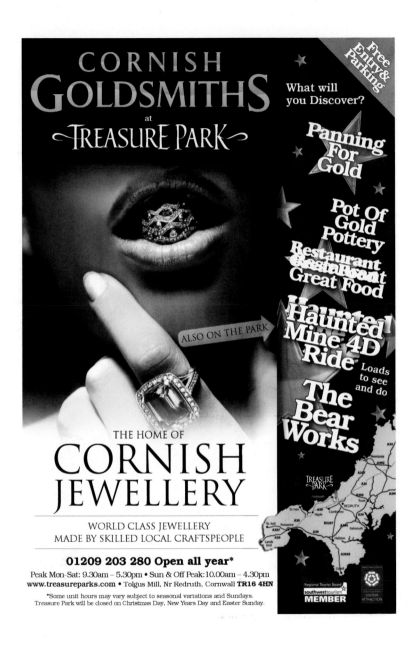

For your wedding day, do you dream about feeling like a princess?

We make it happen...

THE
Penventon
PARK HOTEL
www.penventon.co.uk

CORNWALL
T~ 01209 203000 E~ INFO@PENVENTON.COM